ALPHABET - الحروف الأبجدية

Handwriting Workbook

أَسَد

Lion	ALIF - أ

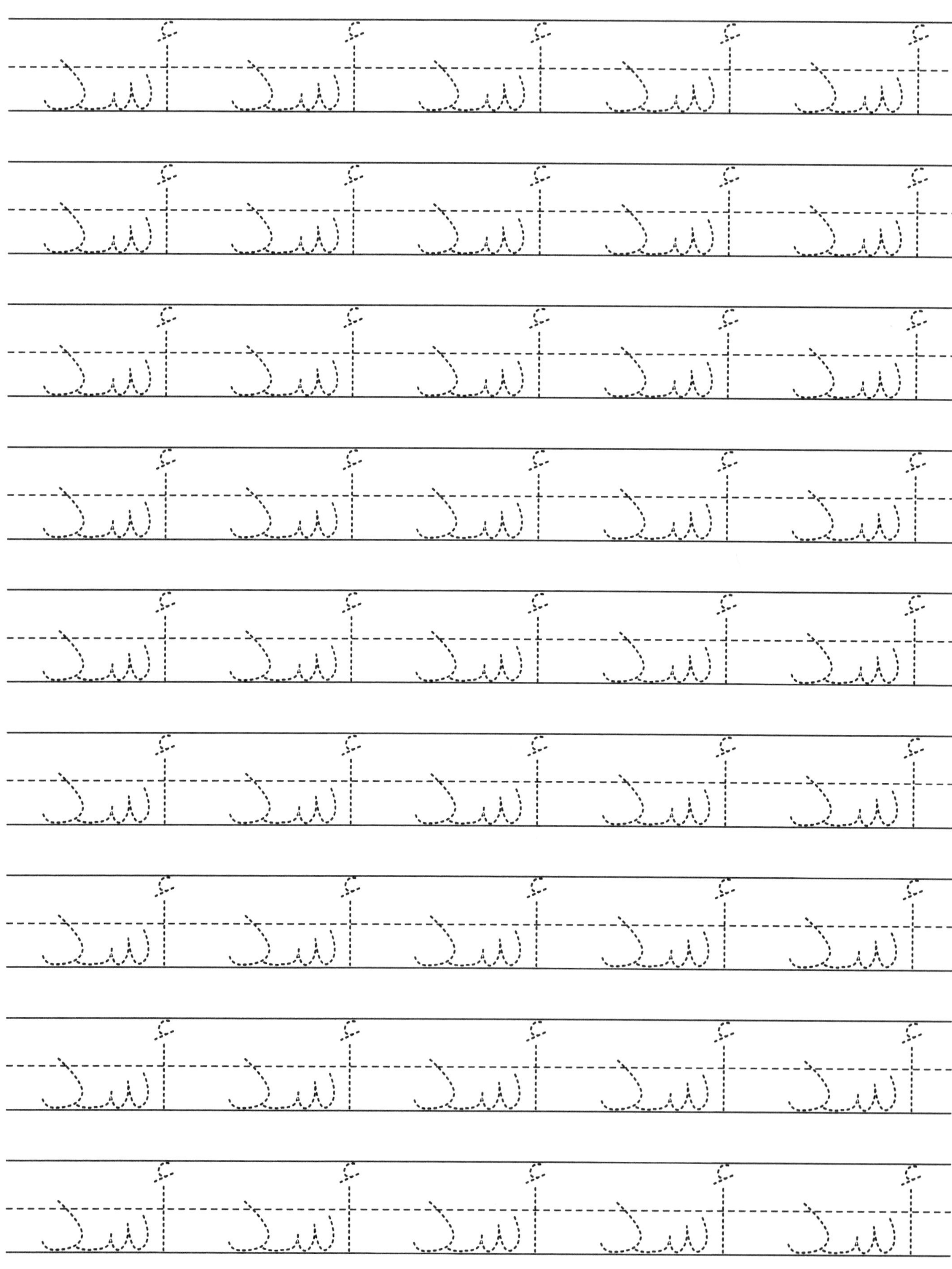

Duck
BAA - ب

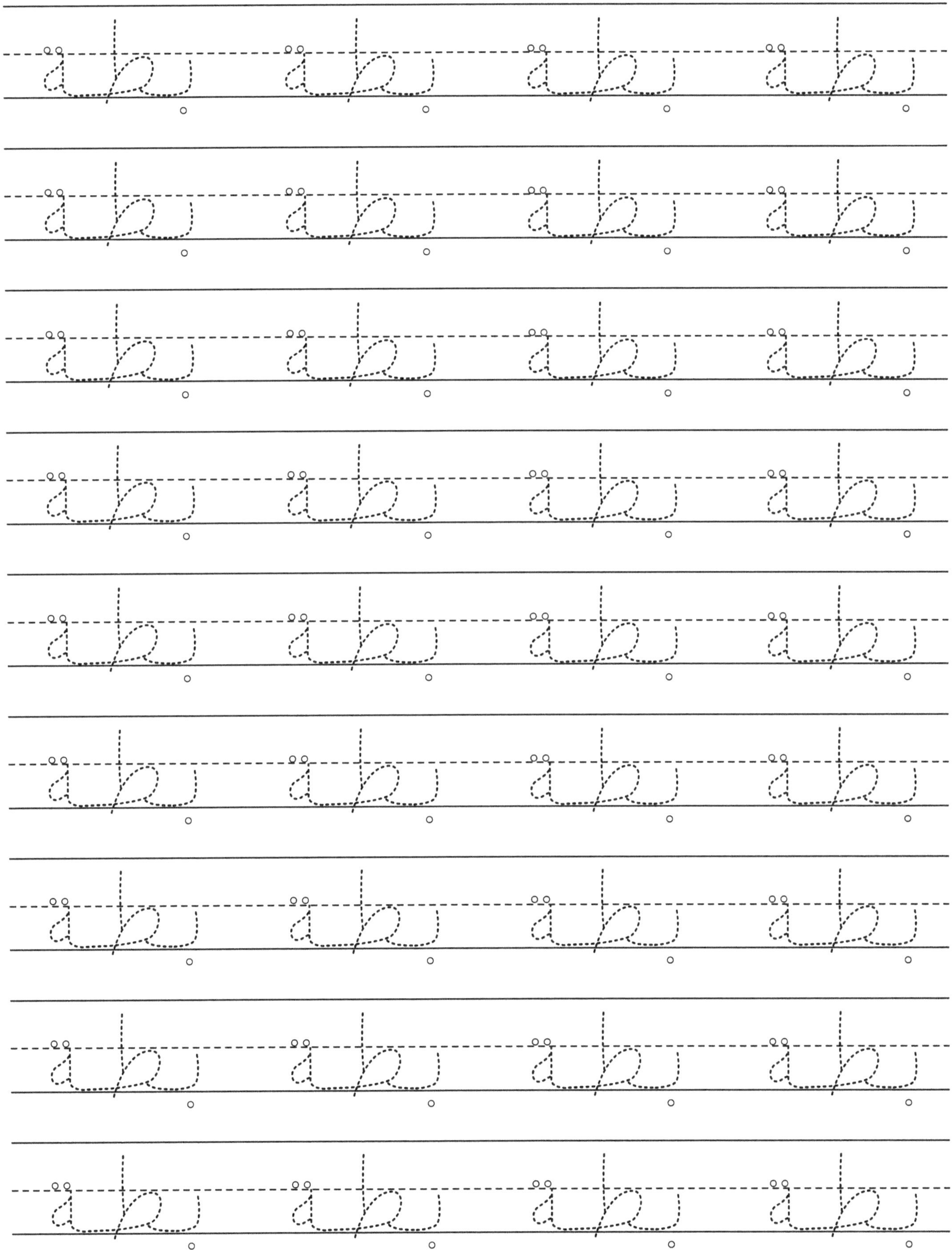

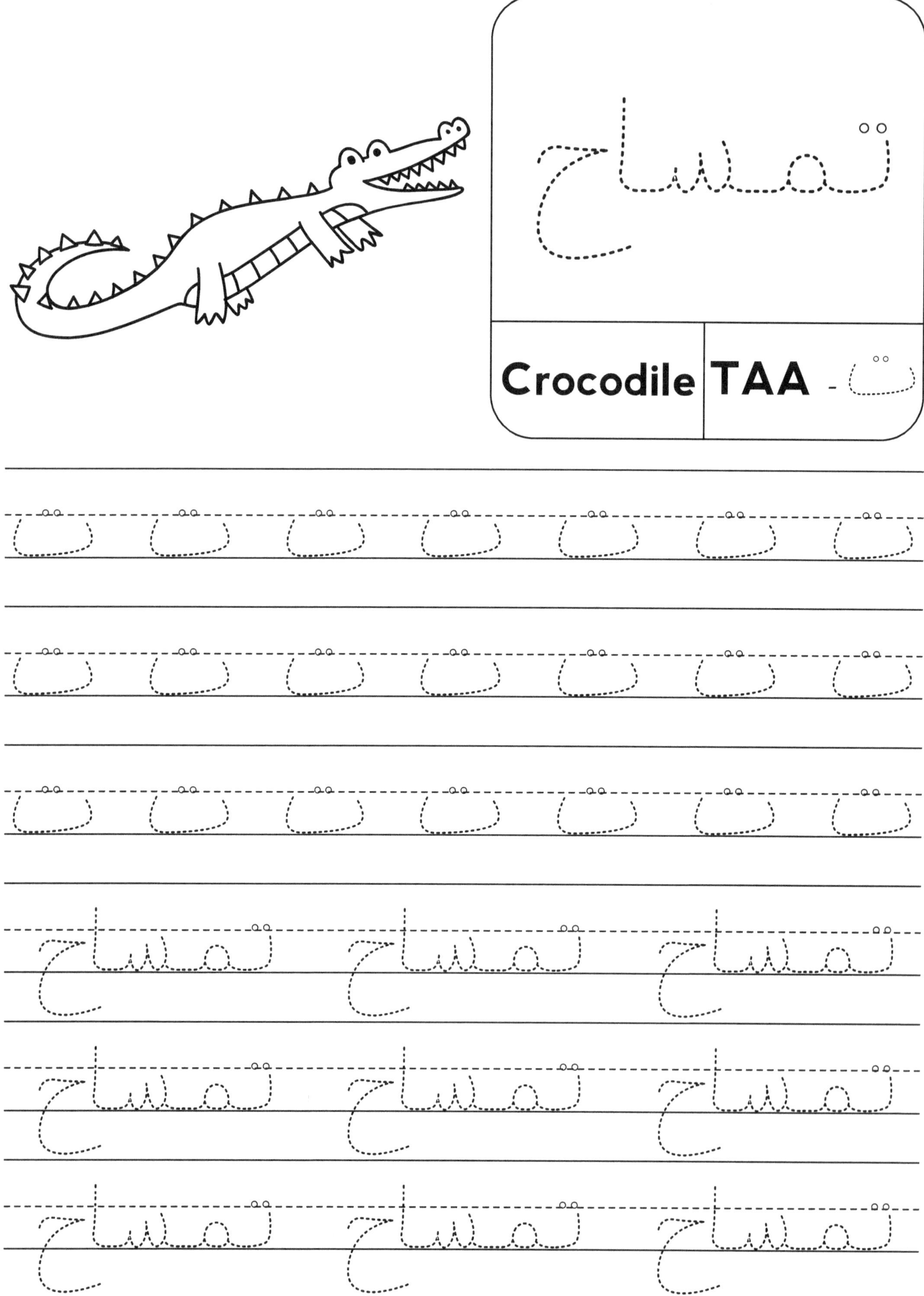

Crocodile
TAA

ثعبان
Snake THAA - ث

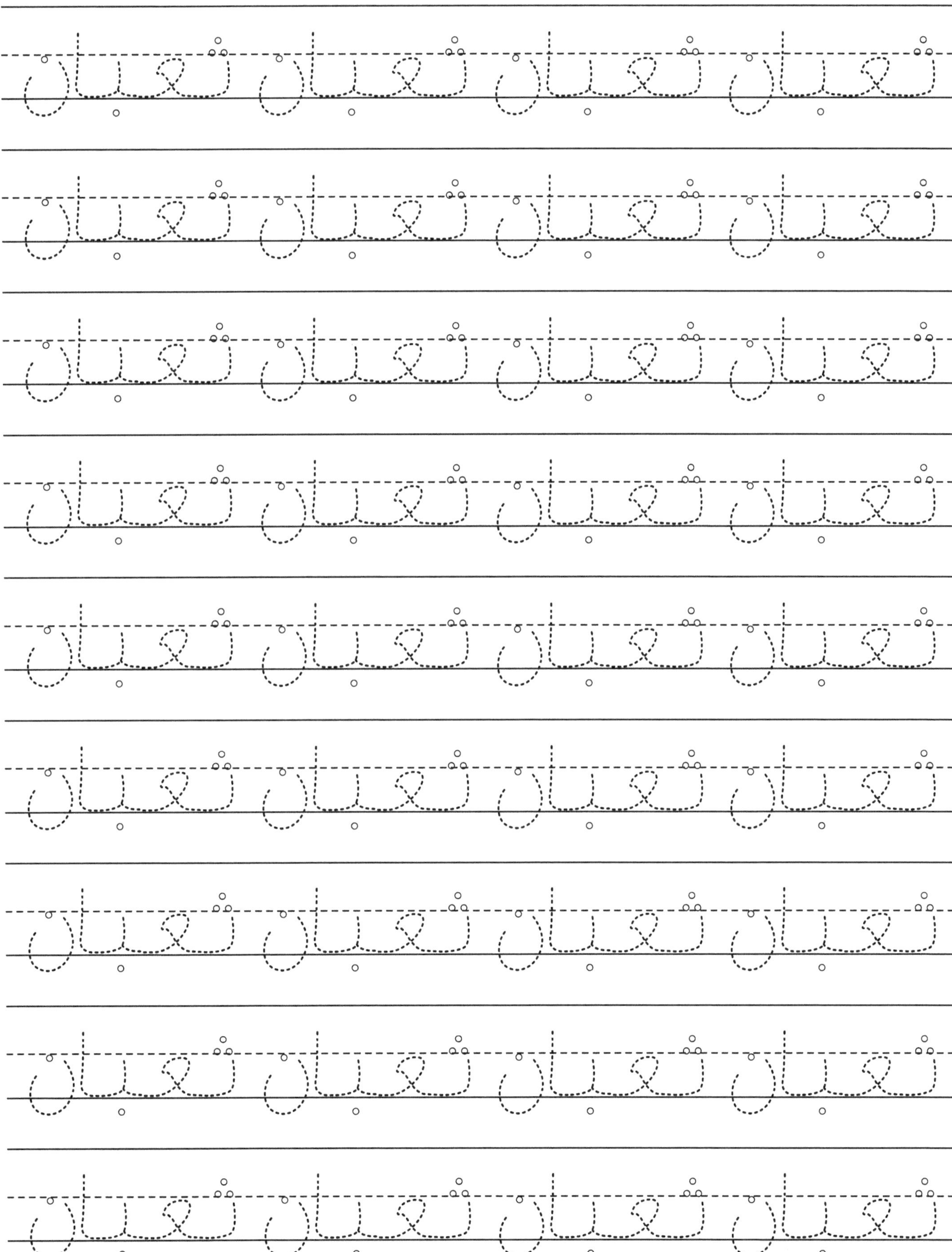

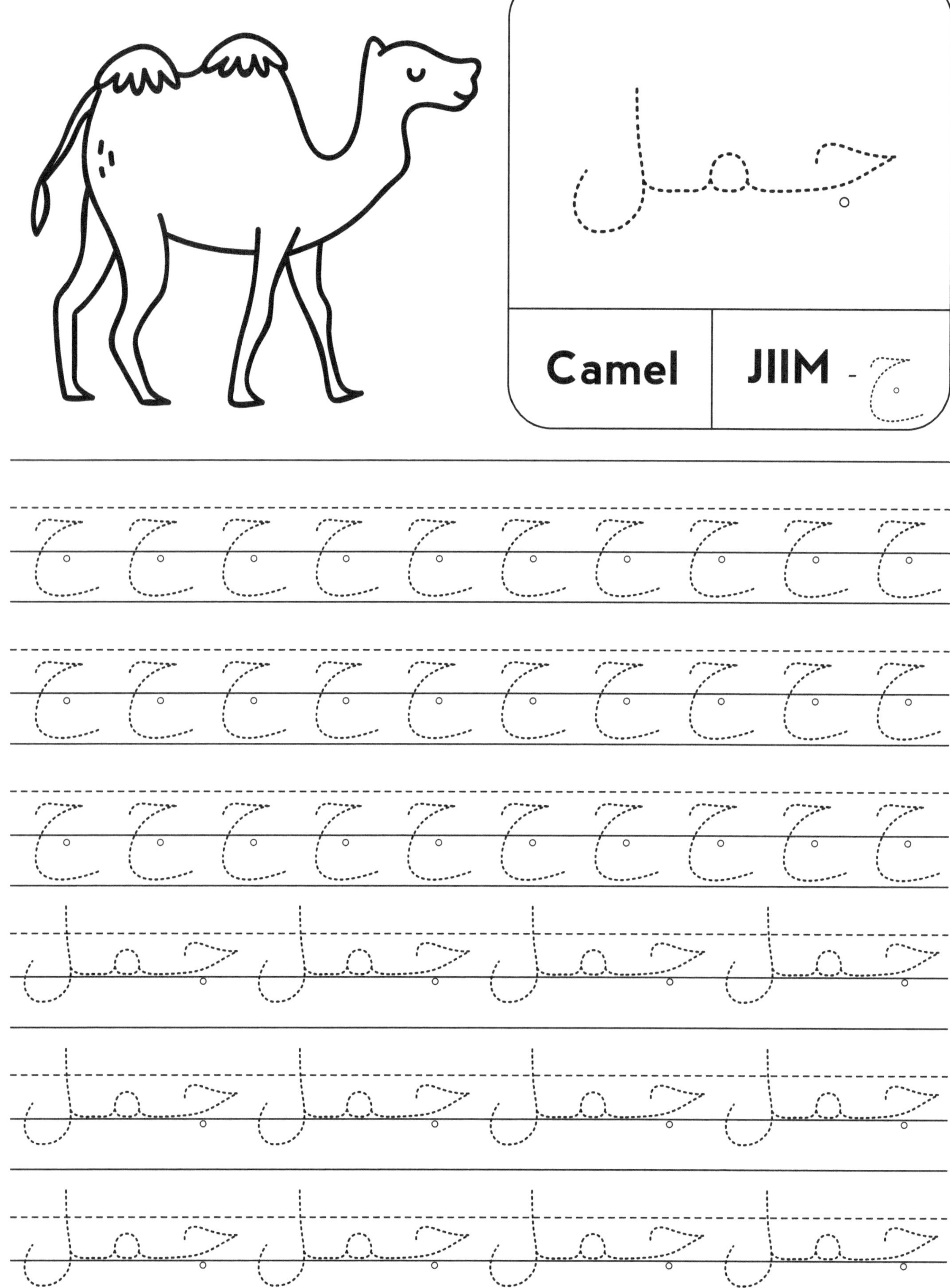

جمـل
Camel
JIIM - ج

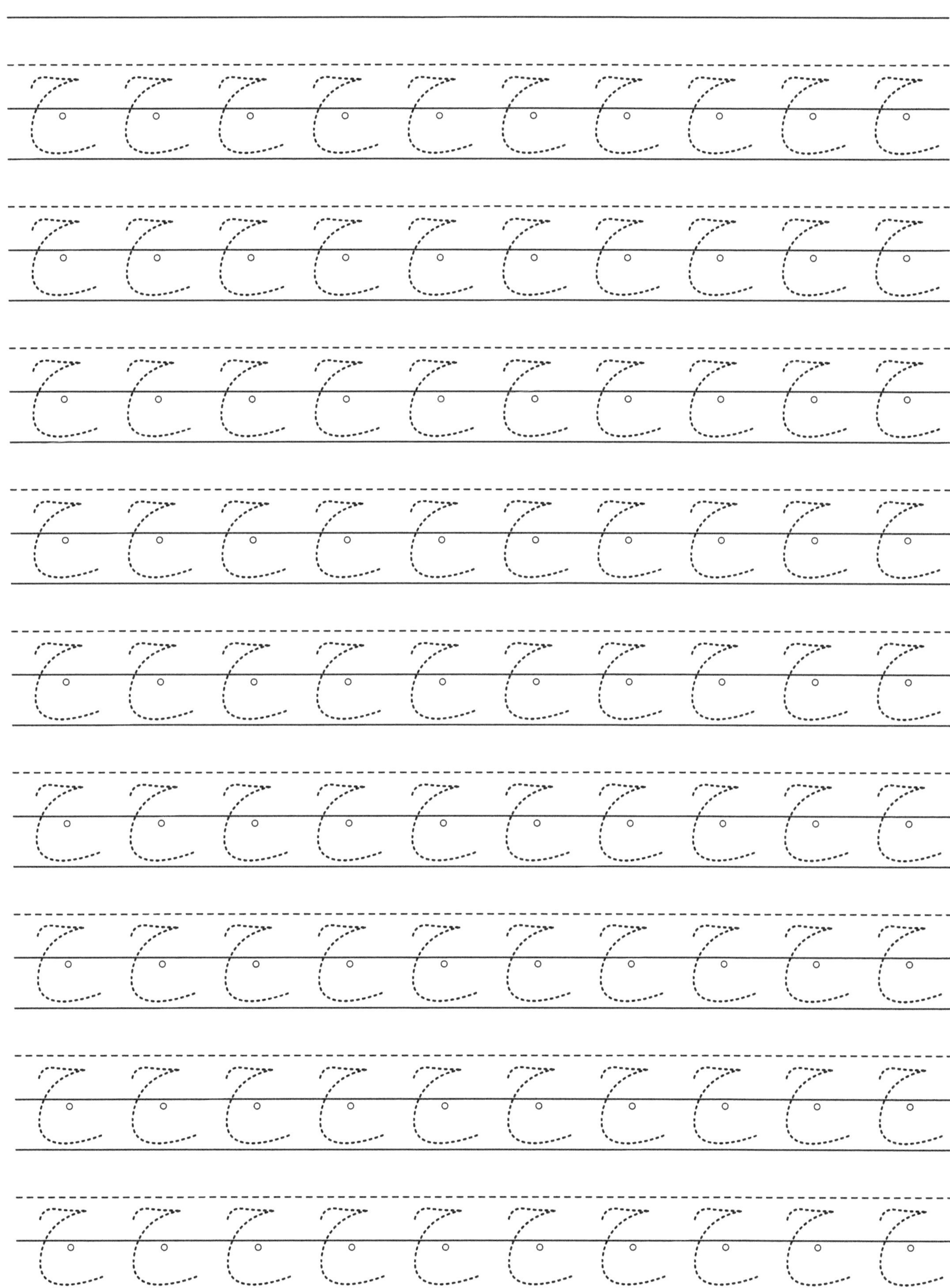

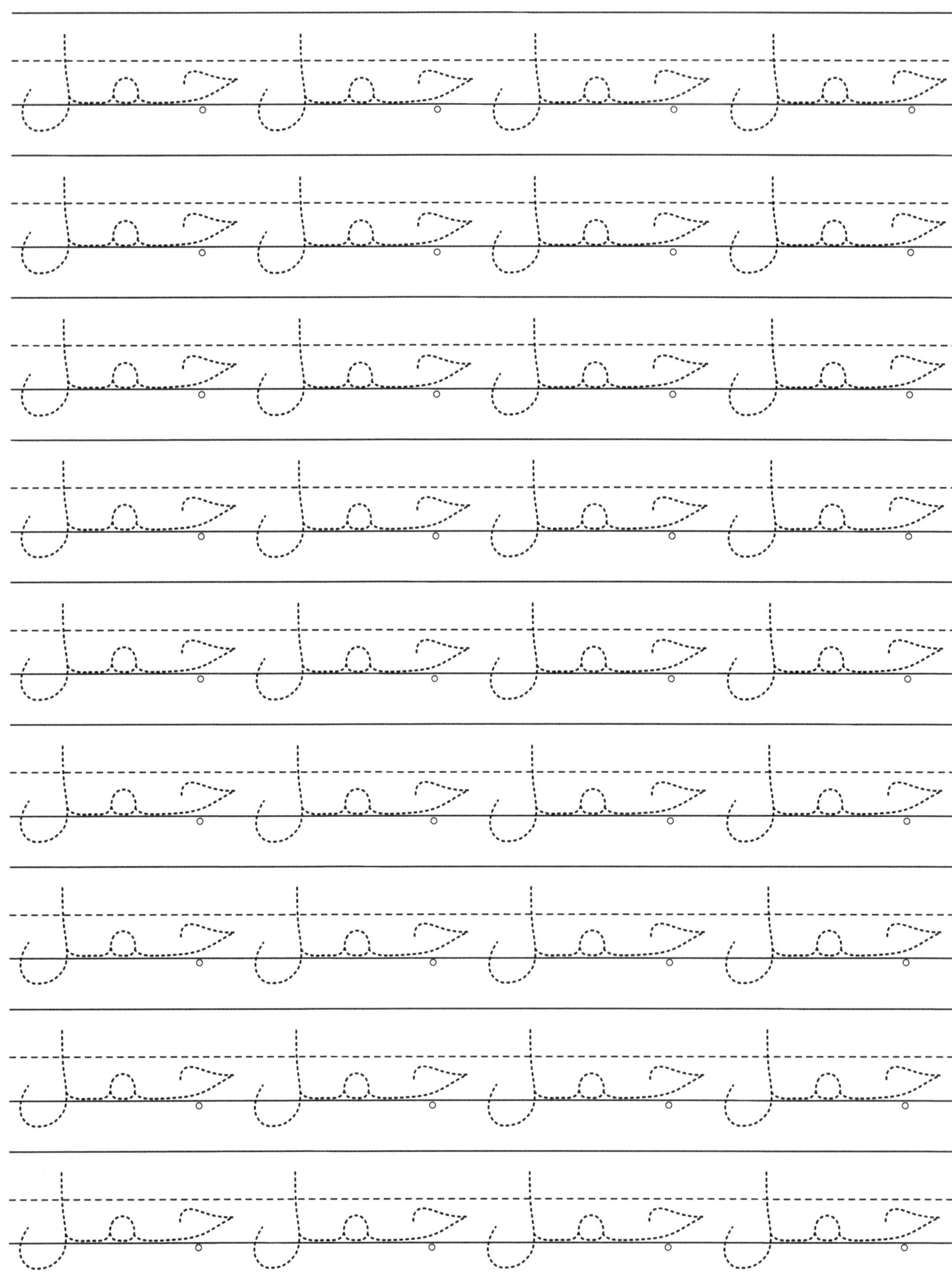

Horse | **HAA - ح**

حصان

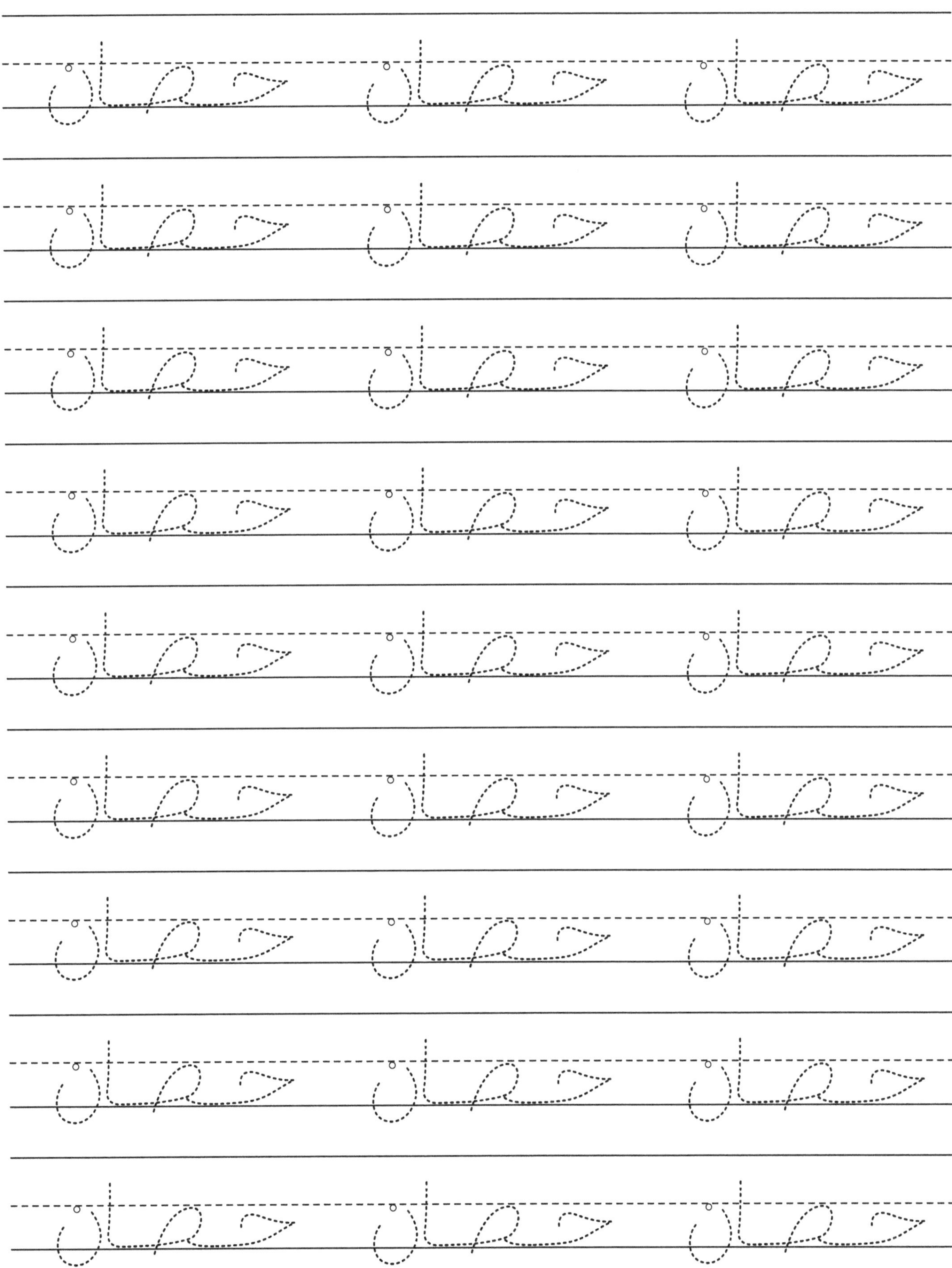

خروف

Sheep | **KHAA** - خ

خ خ خ خ خ خ خ خ خ خ

خ خ خ خ خ خ خ خ خ خ

خ خ خ خ خ خ خ خ خ خ

خروف خروف خروف

خروف خروف خروف

خروف خروف خروف

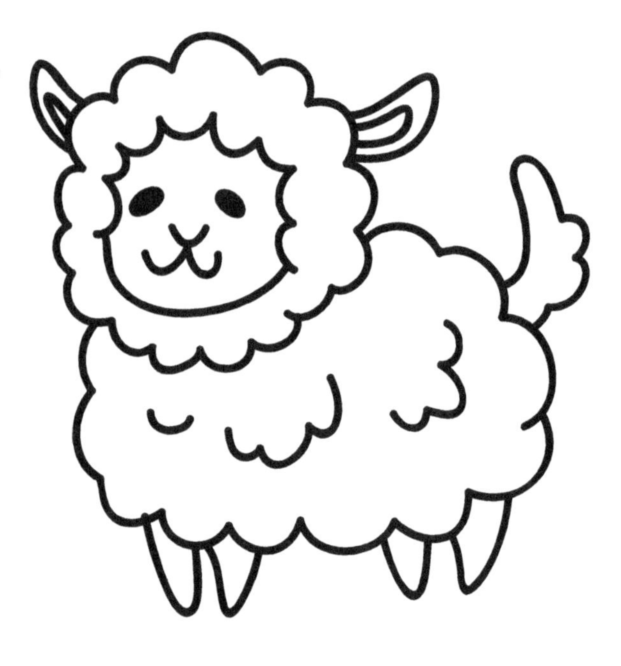

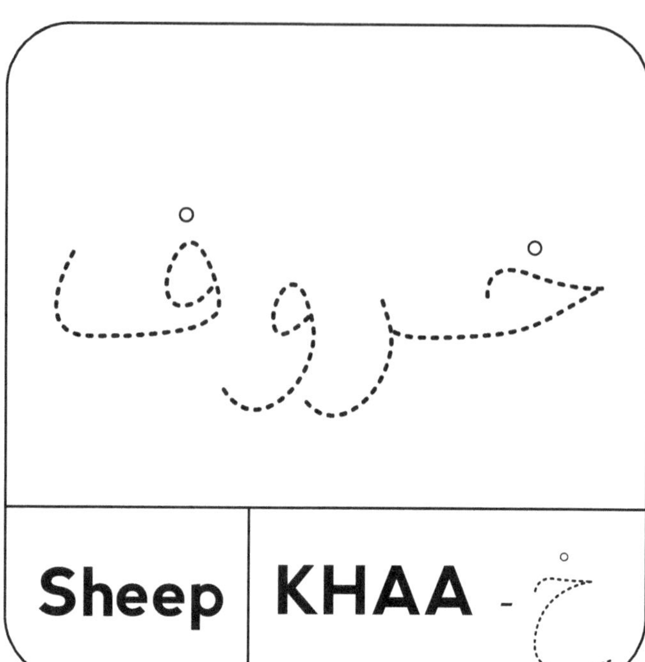

ـبـ
Bear
DAAL - ـد

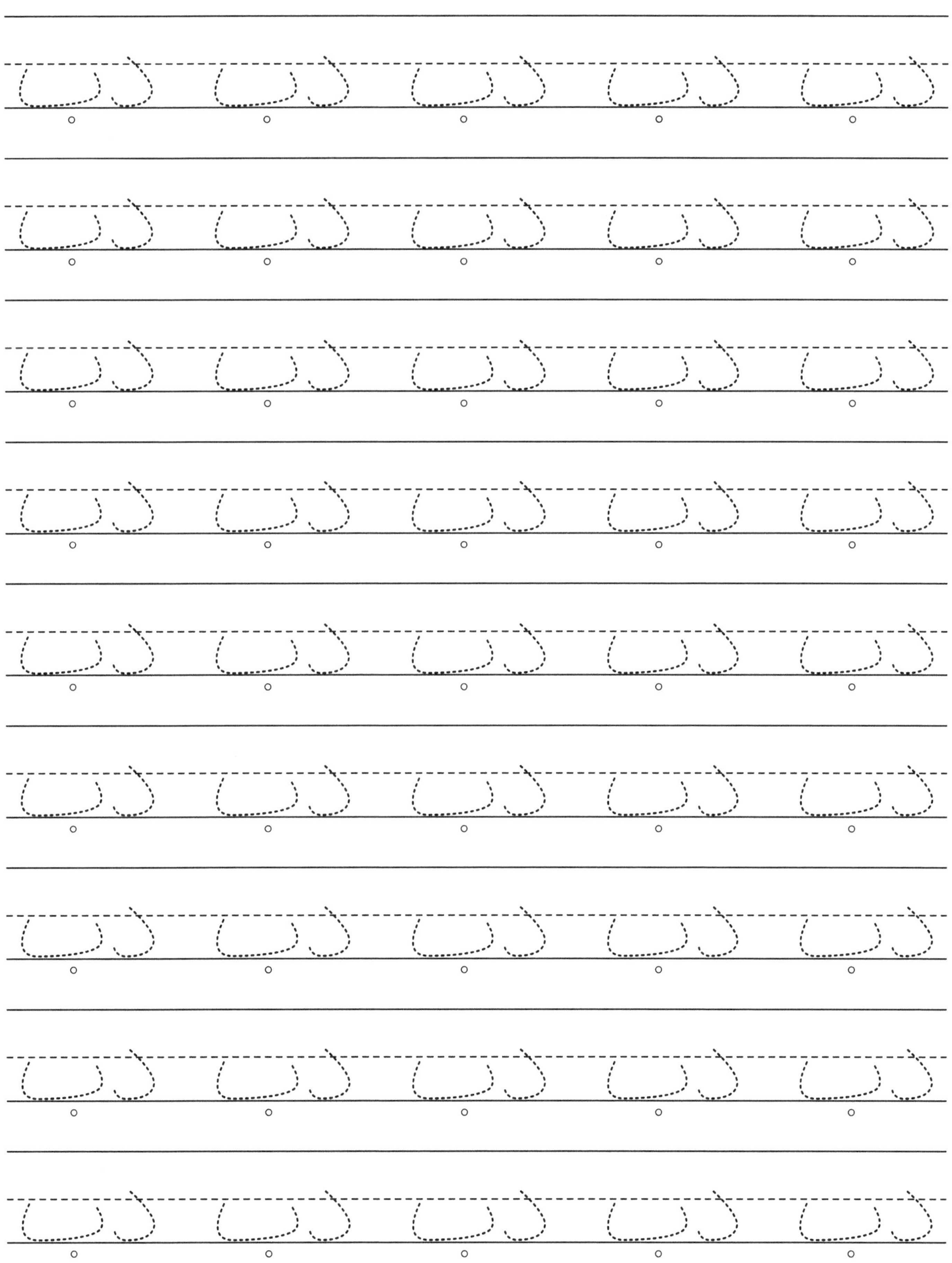

ذئب

Wolf	DHAAL - ذ

ذ ذ ذ ذ ذ ذ ذ ذ ذ ذ ذ

ذ ذ ذ ذ ذ ذ ذ ذ ذ ذ ذ

ذ ذ ذ ذ ذ ذ ذ ذ ذ ذ ذ

ذئب ذئب ذئب ذئب

ذئب ذئب ذئب ذئب

ذئب ذئب ذئب ذئب

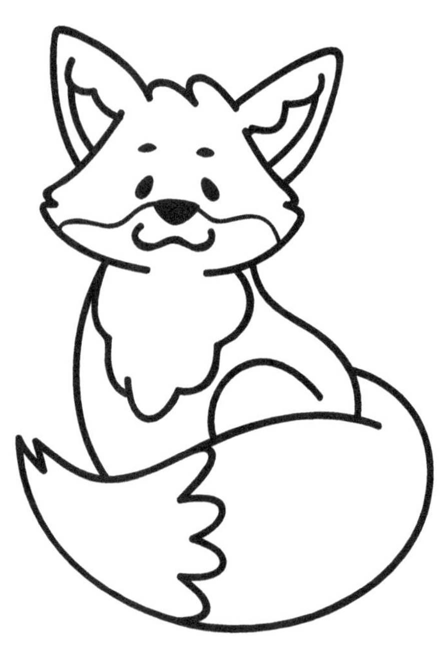

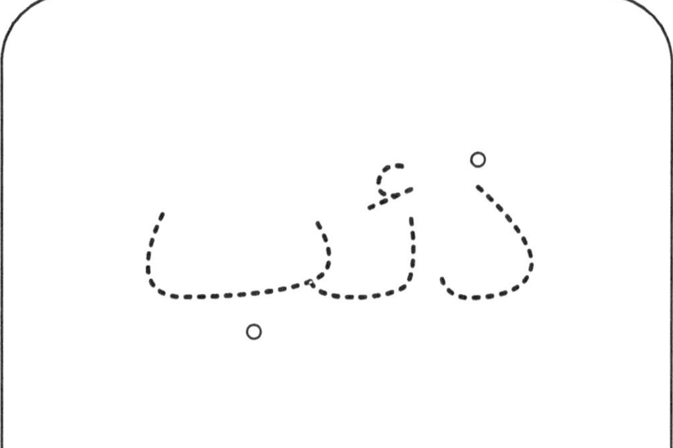

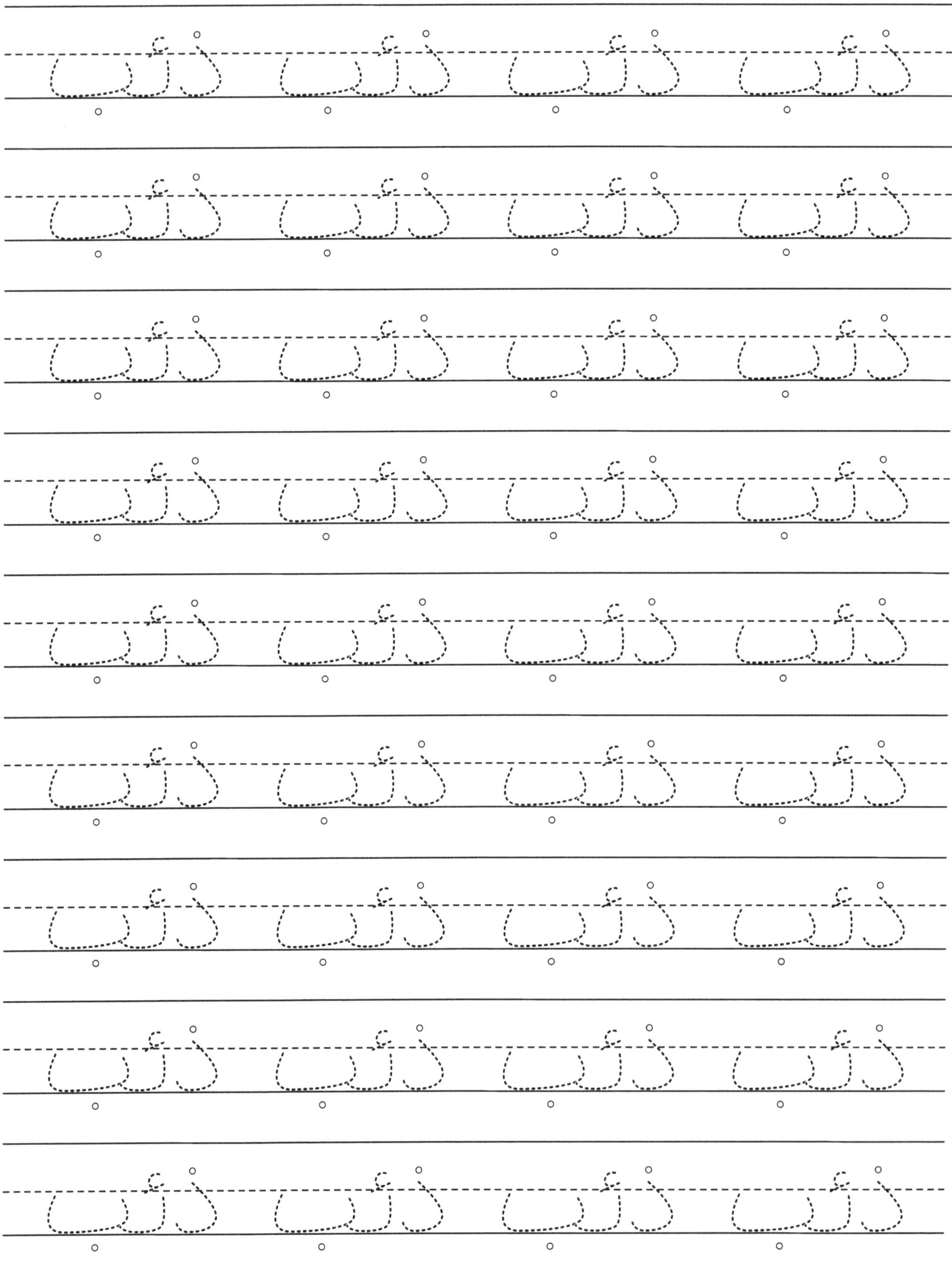

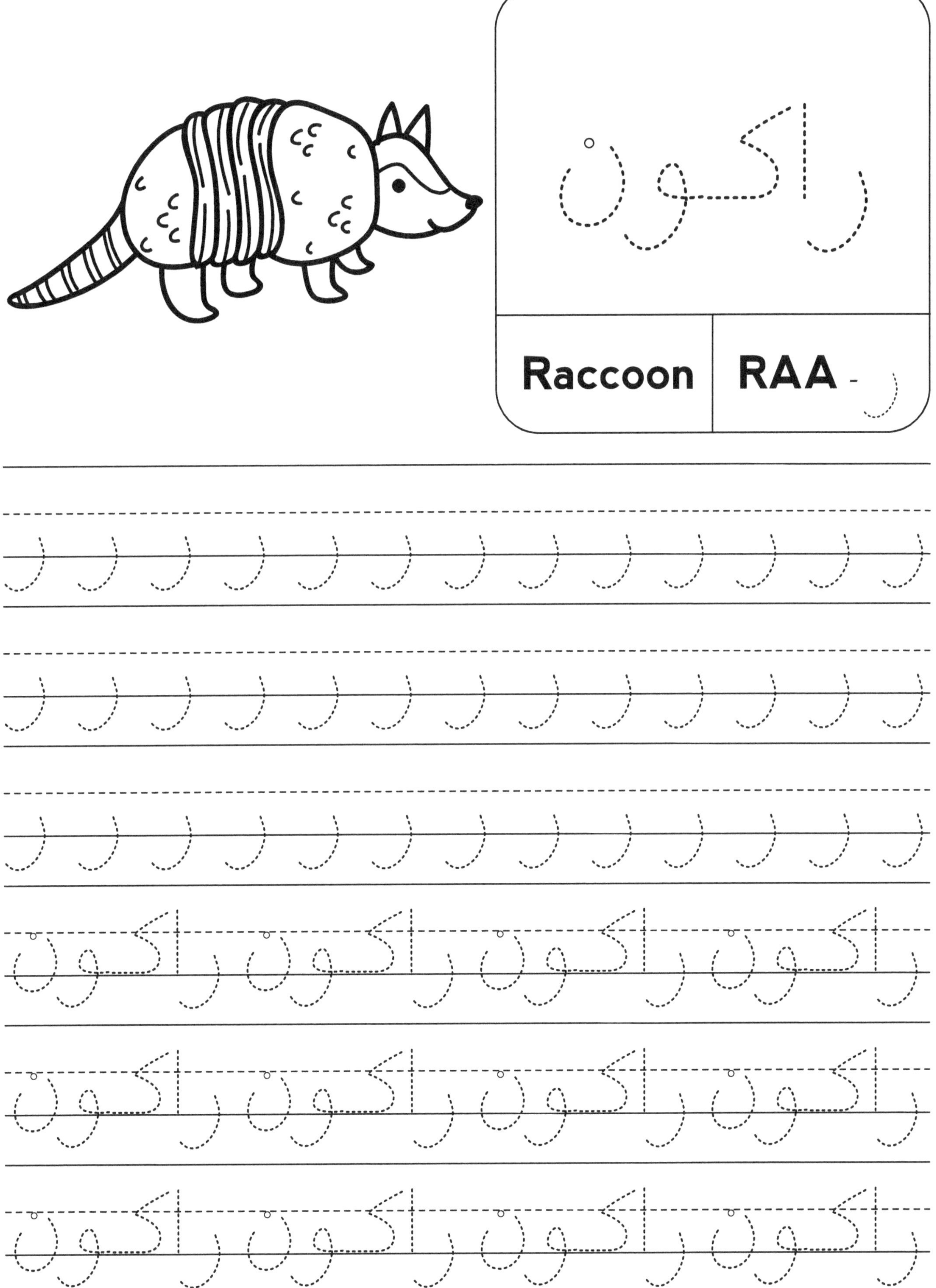
راكون
Raccoon
RAA -

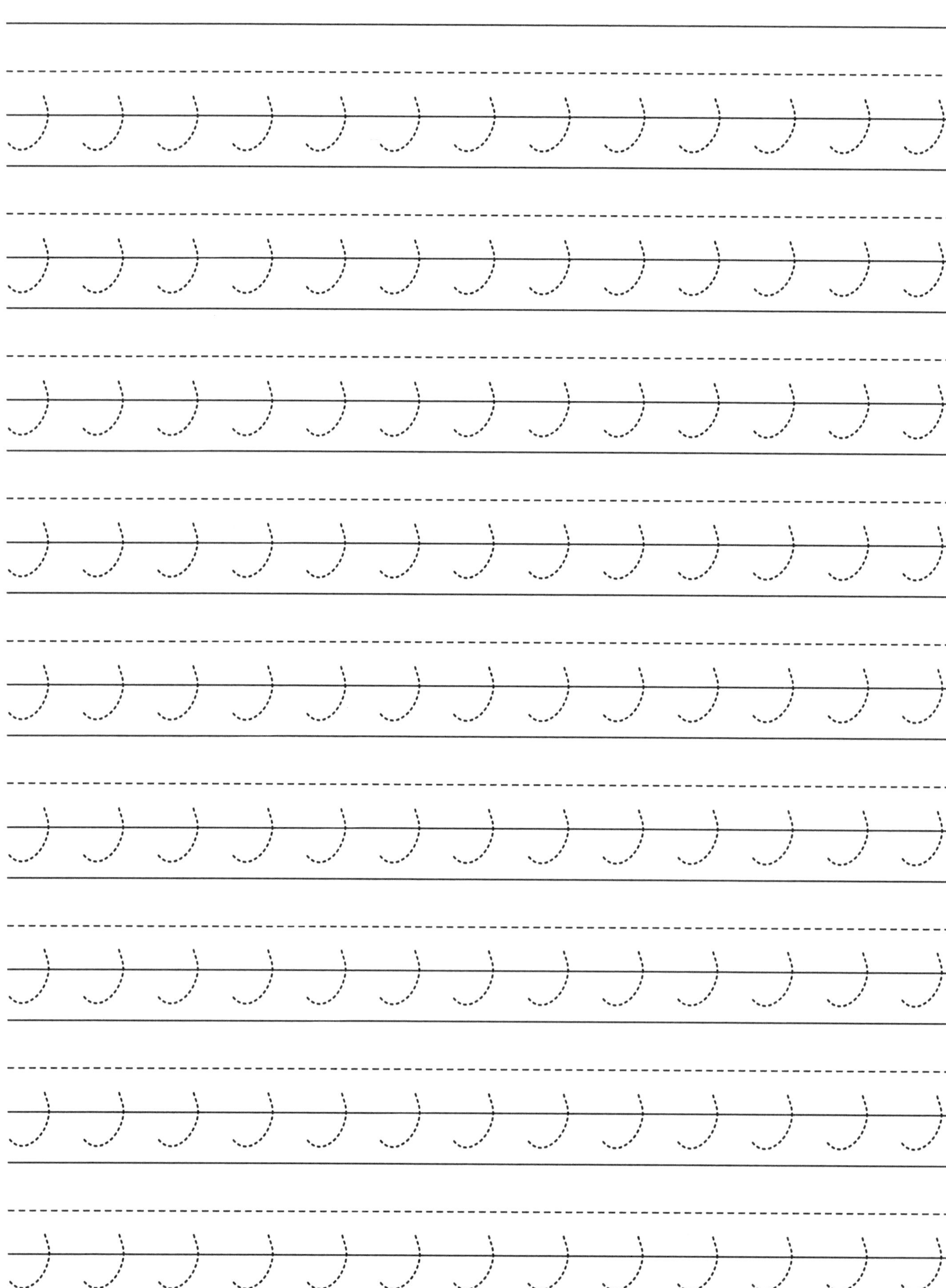

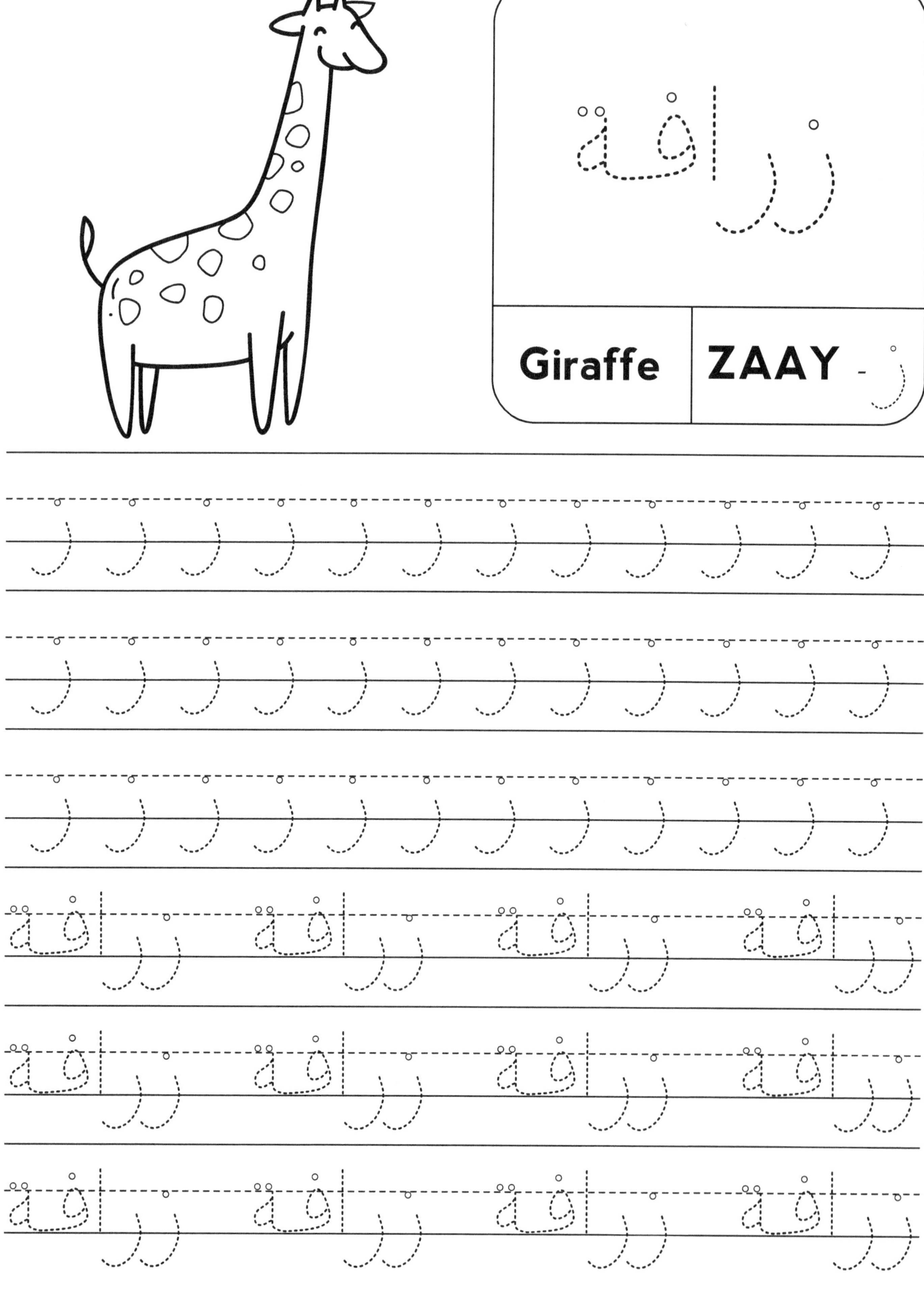

زَرَافَة
Giraffe
ZAAY - ز

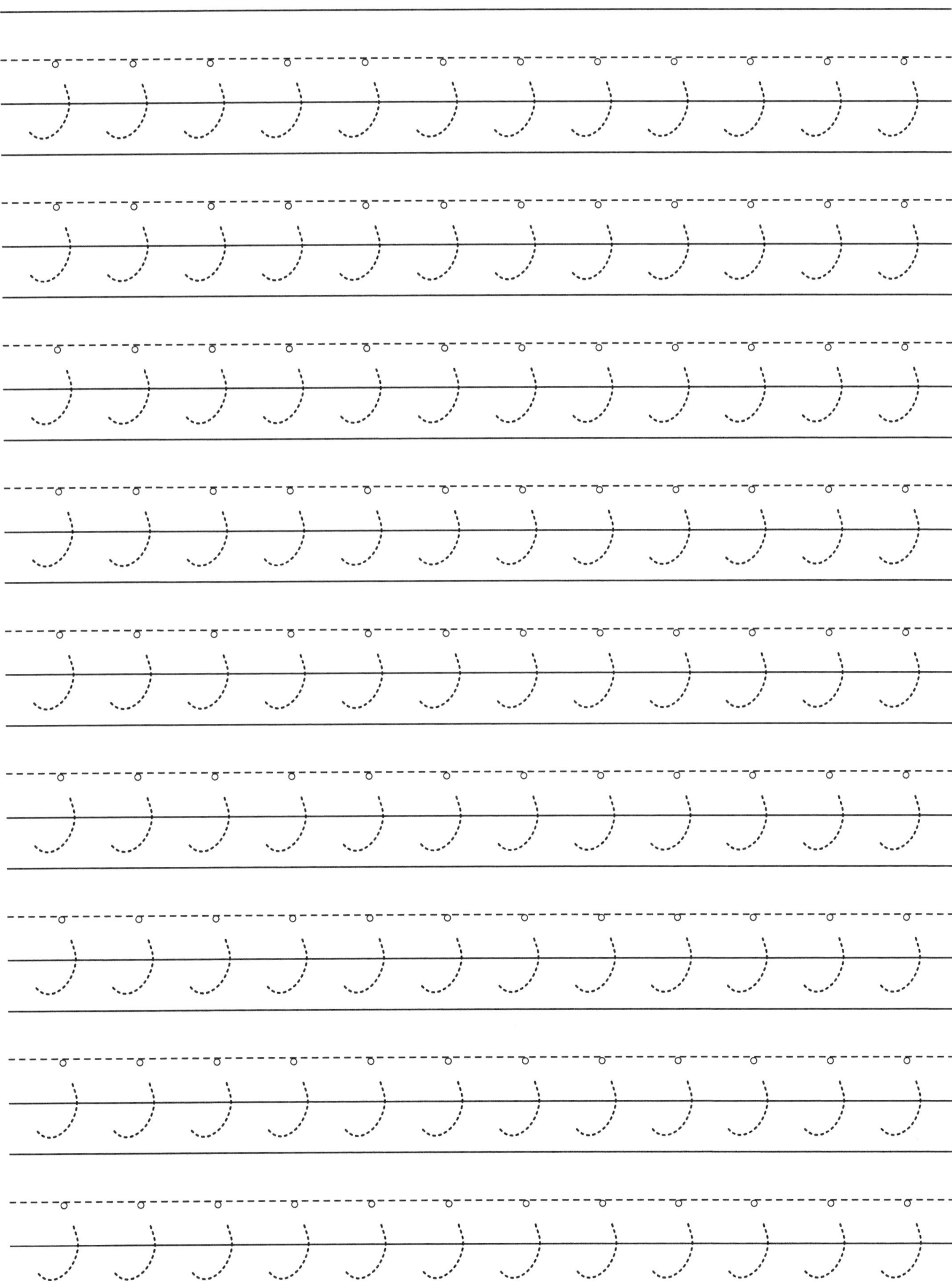

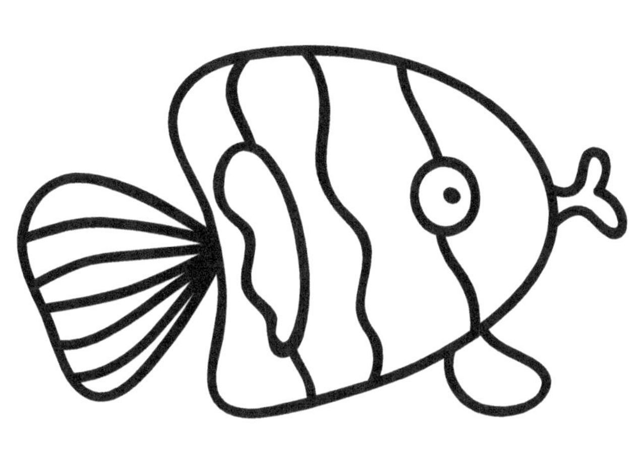

سمكة

Fish	SIIN - س

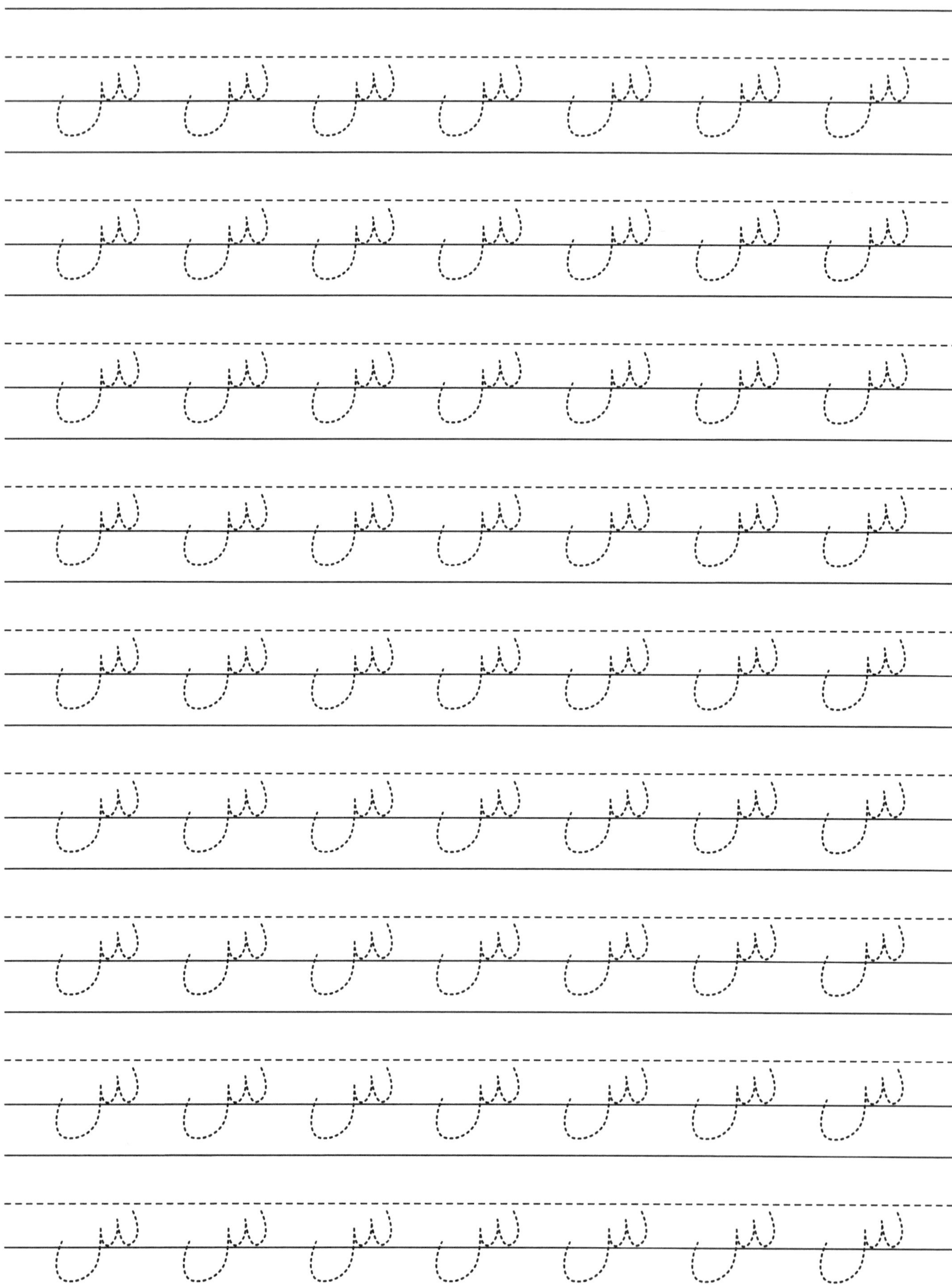

Saw Saw Saw

Saw Saw Saw

Saw Saw Saw

Saw Saw Saw

Saw Saw Saw

Saw Saw Saw

Saw Saw Saw

Saw Saw Saw

Saw Saw Saw

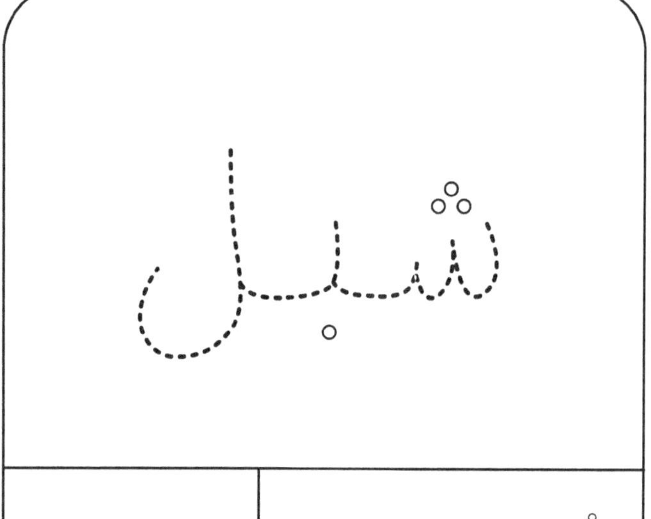

شِبْل
Cub
SHIIN - شْ

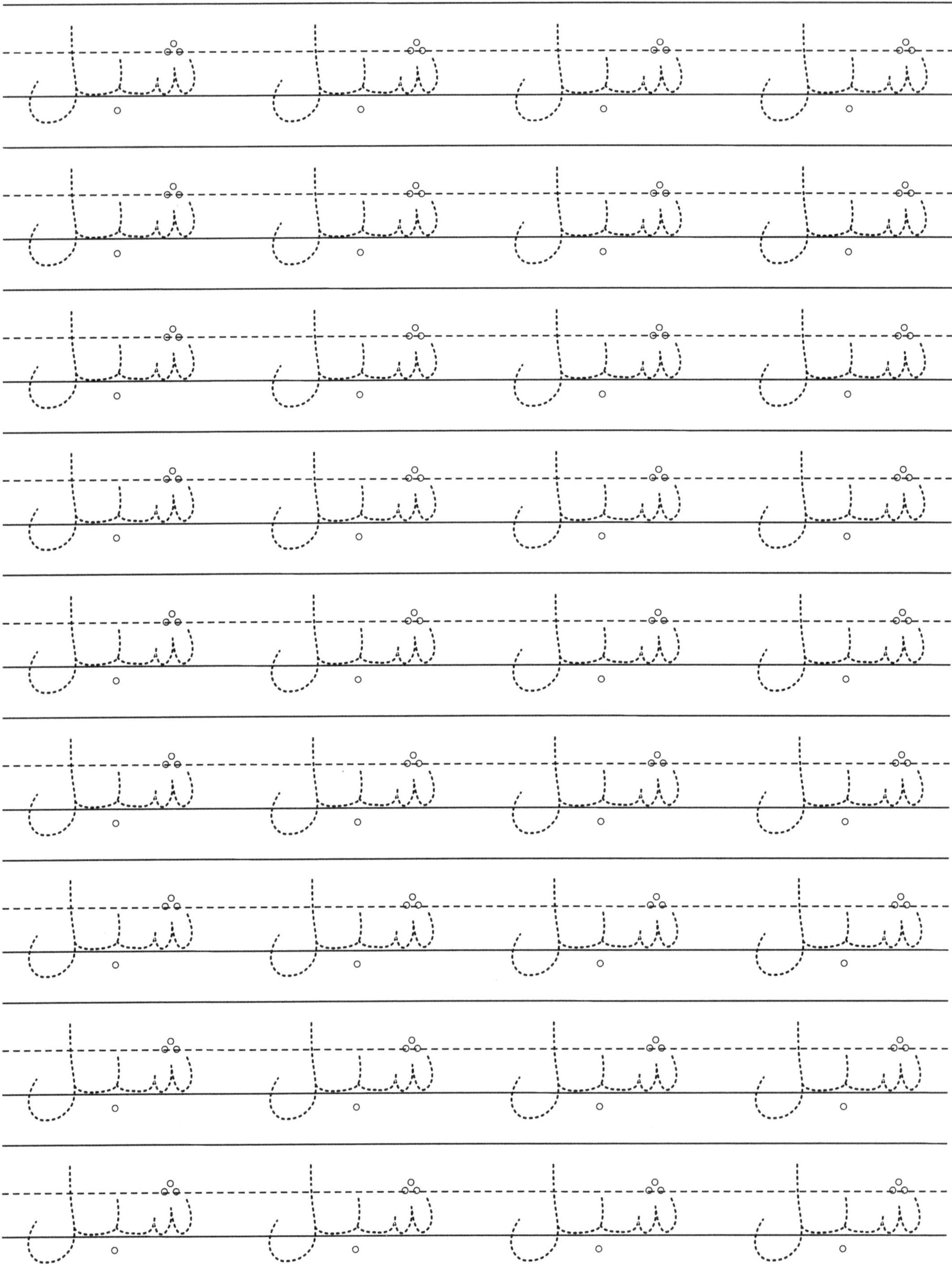

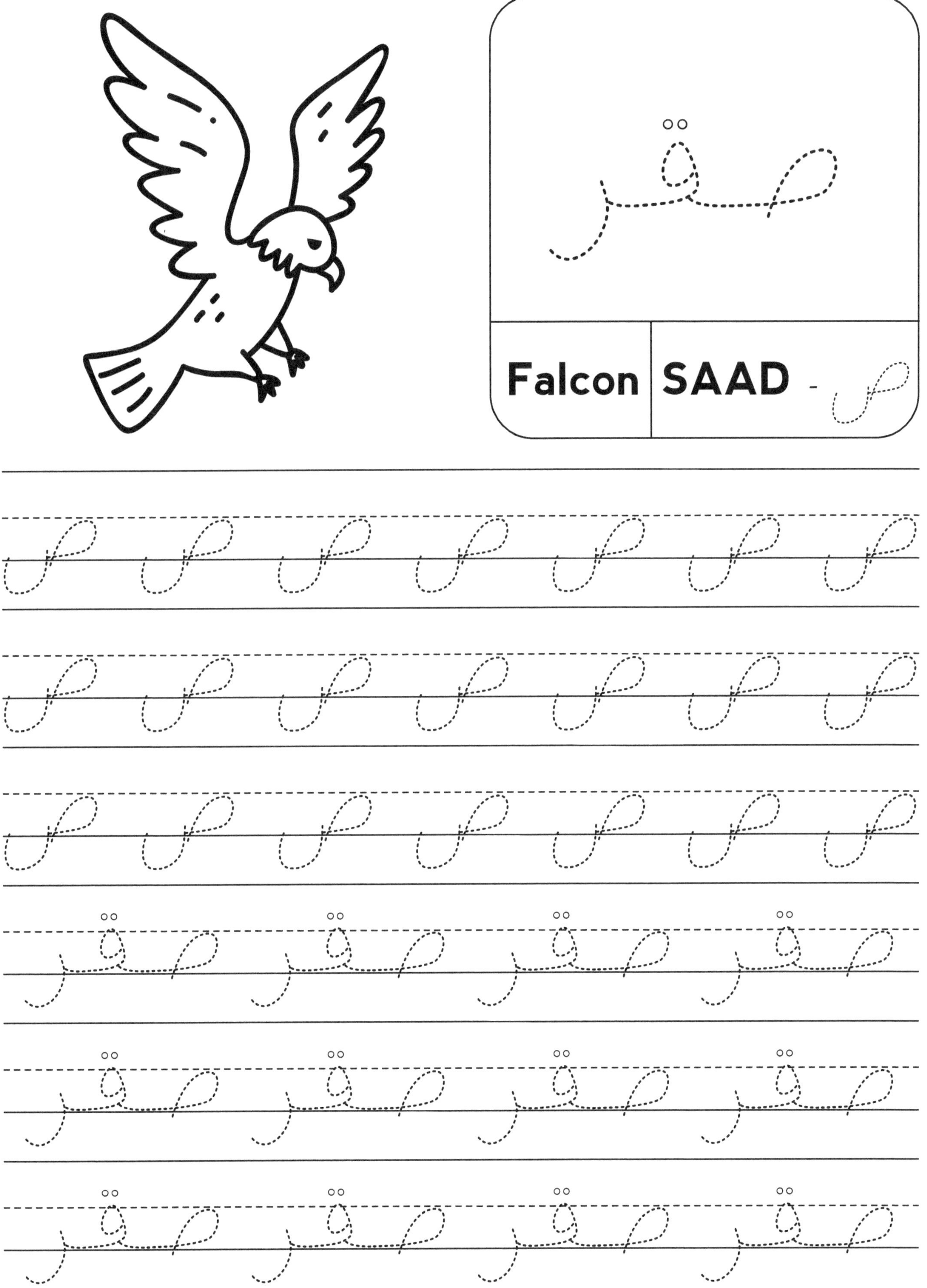

Falcon | SAAD -

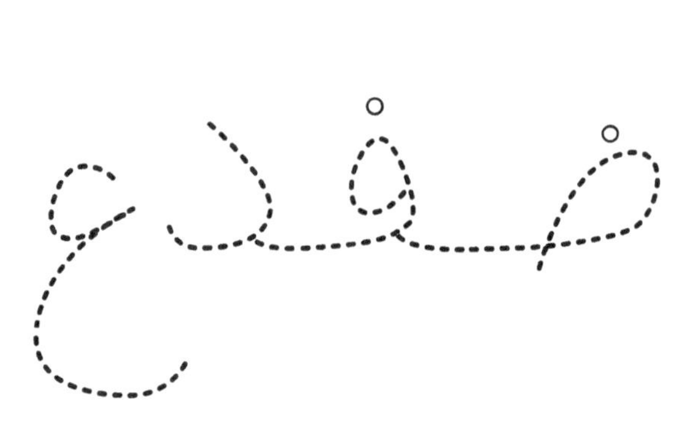

Frog | **DAAD** -

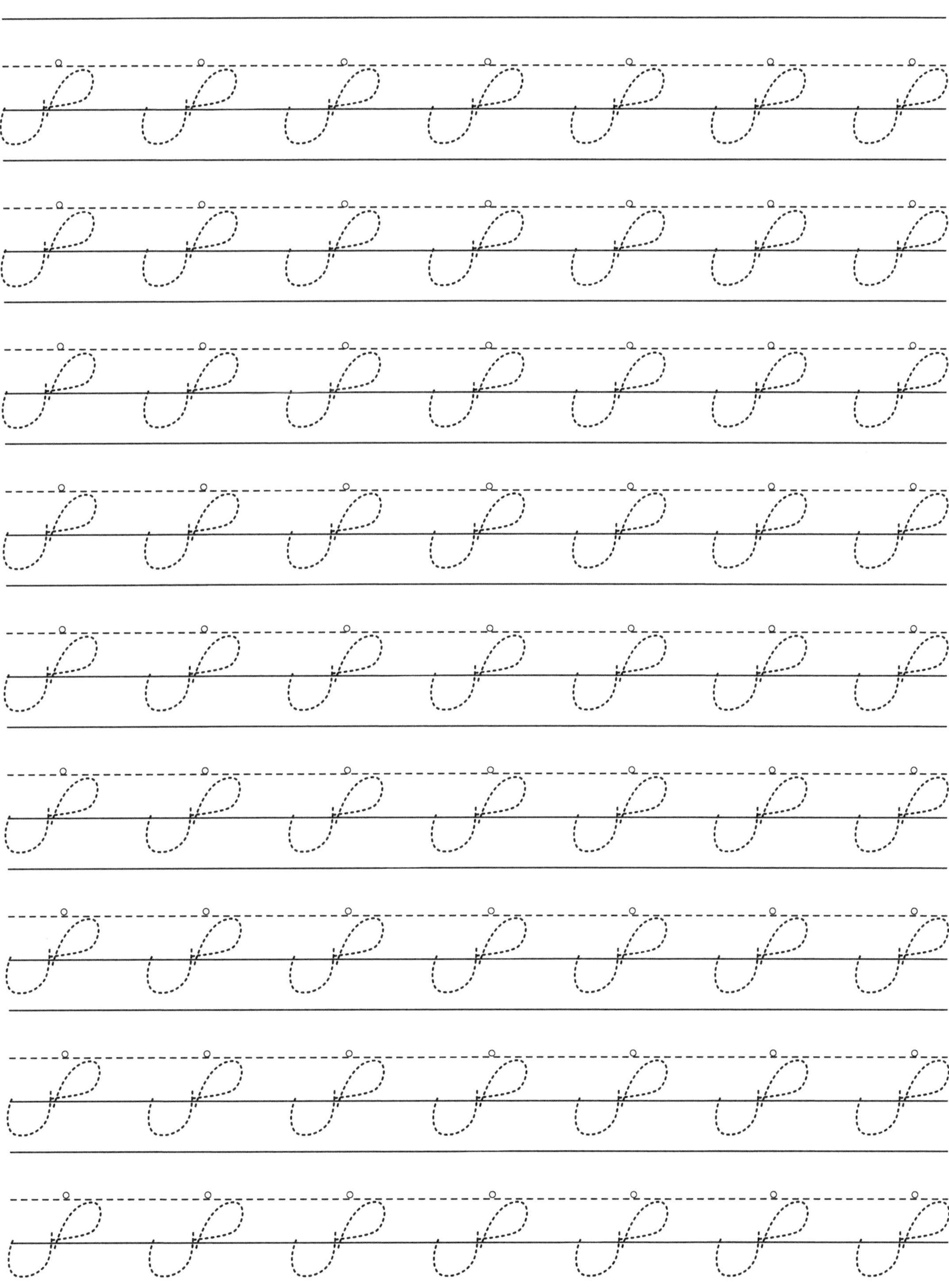

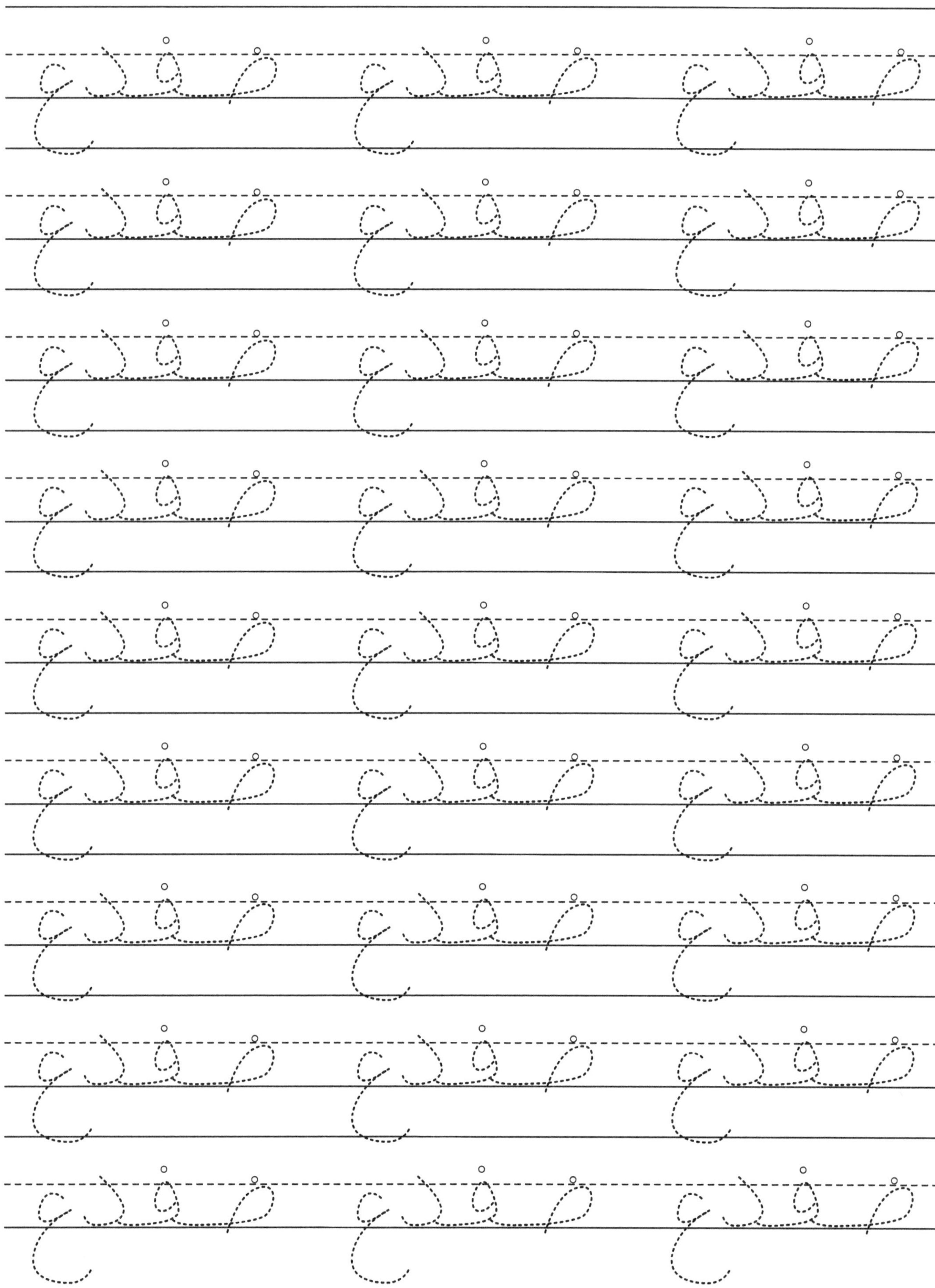

طاووس

Peacock | **TAA** - ط

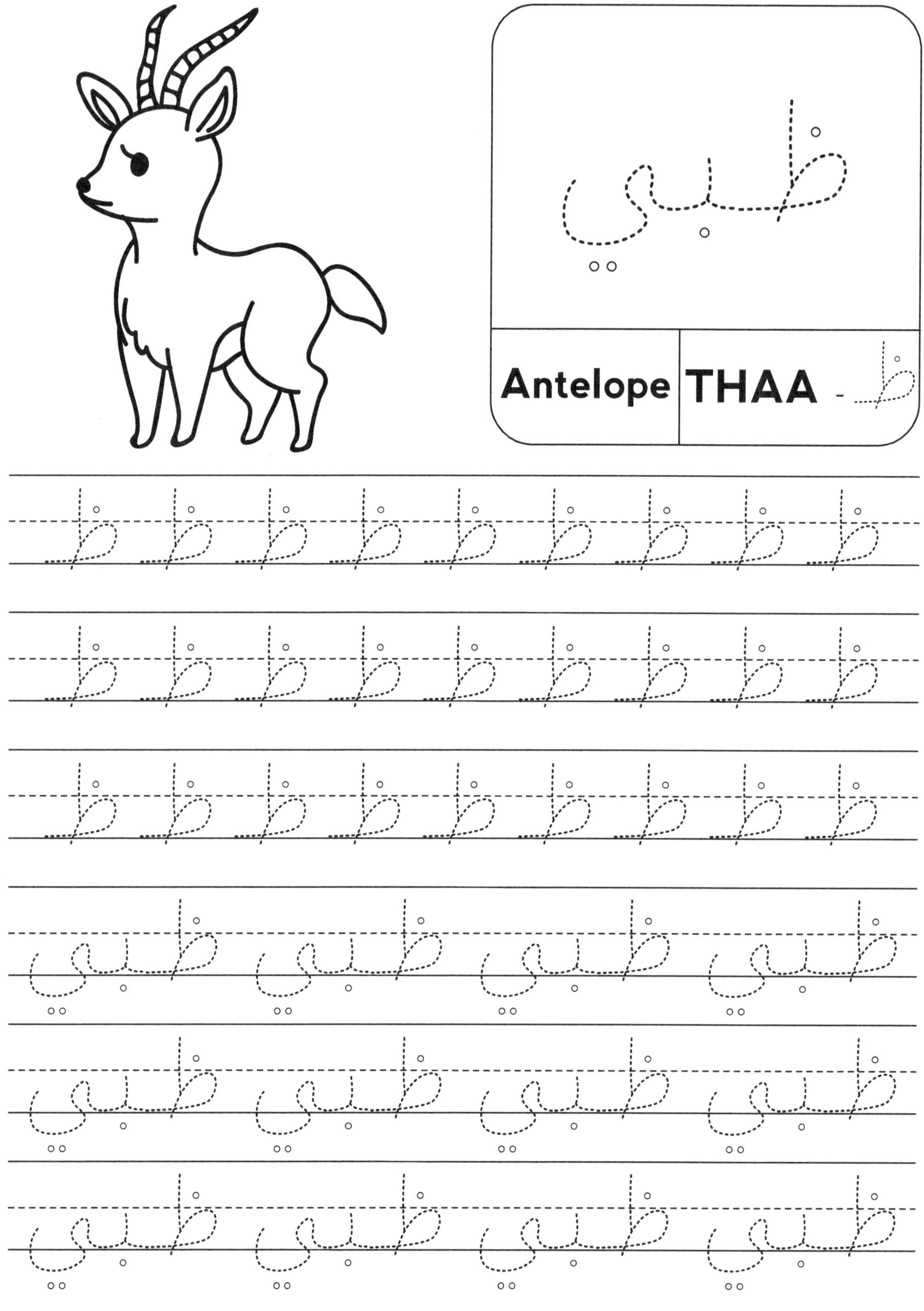

Antelope
THAA

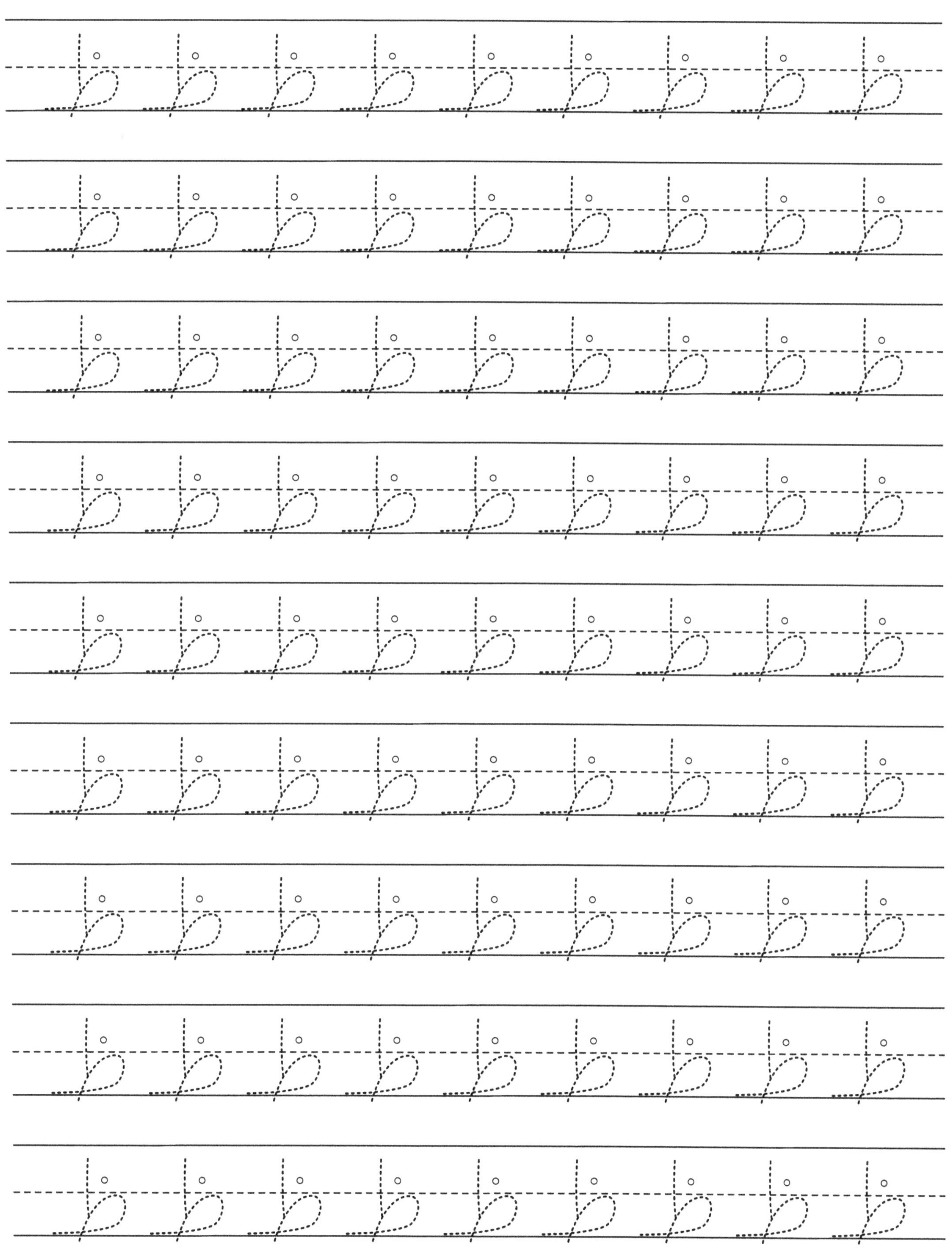

عصفور

Bird | **AIN** - ع

ع ع ع ع ع ع ع ع ع ع ع ع ع

ع ع ع ع ع ع ع ع ع ع ع ع ع

ع ع ع ع ع ع ع ع ع ع ع ع ع

عصفور عصفور عصفور

عصفور عصفور عصفور

عصفور عصفور عصفور

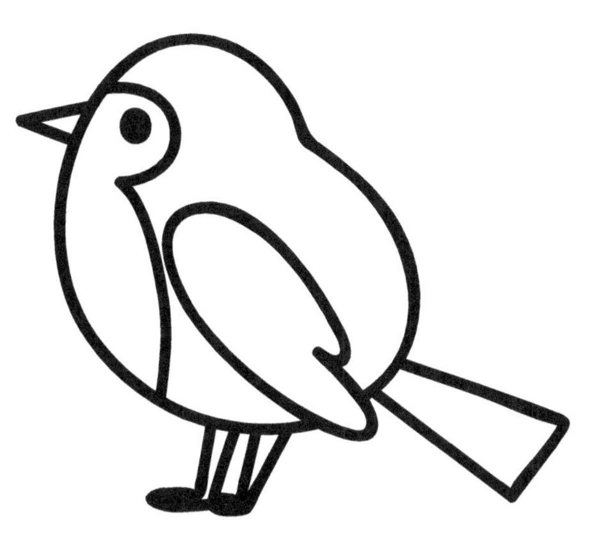

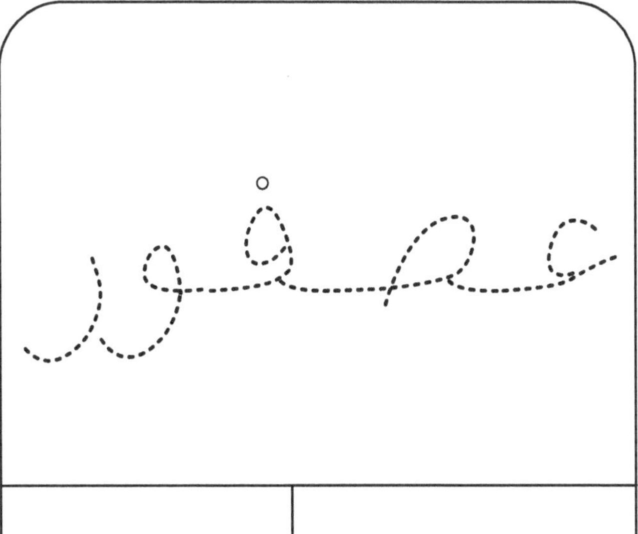

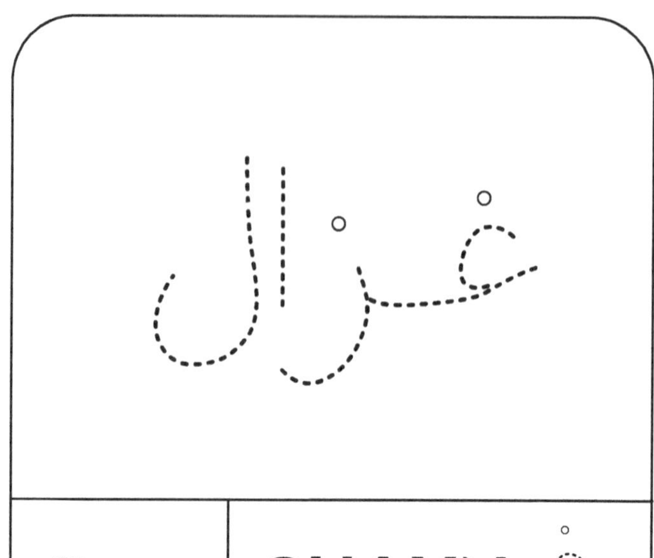

Deer | **GHAYN -** غ

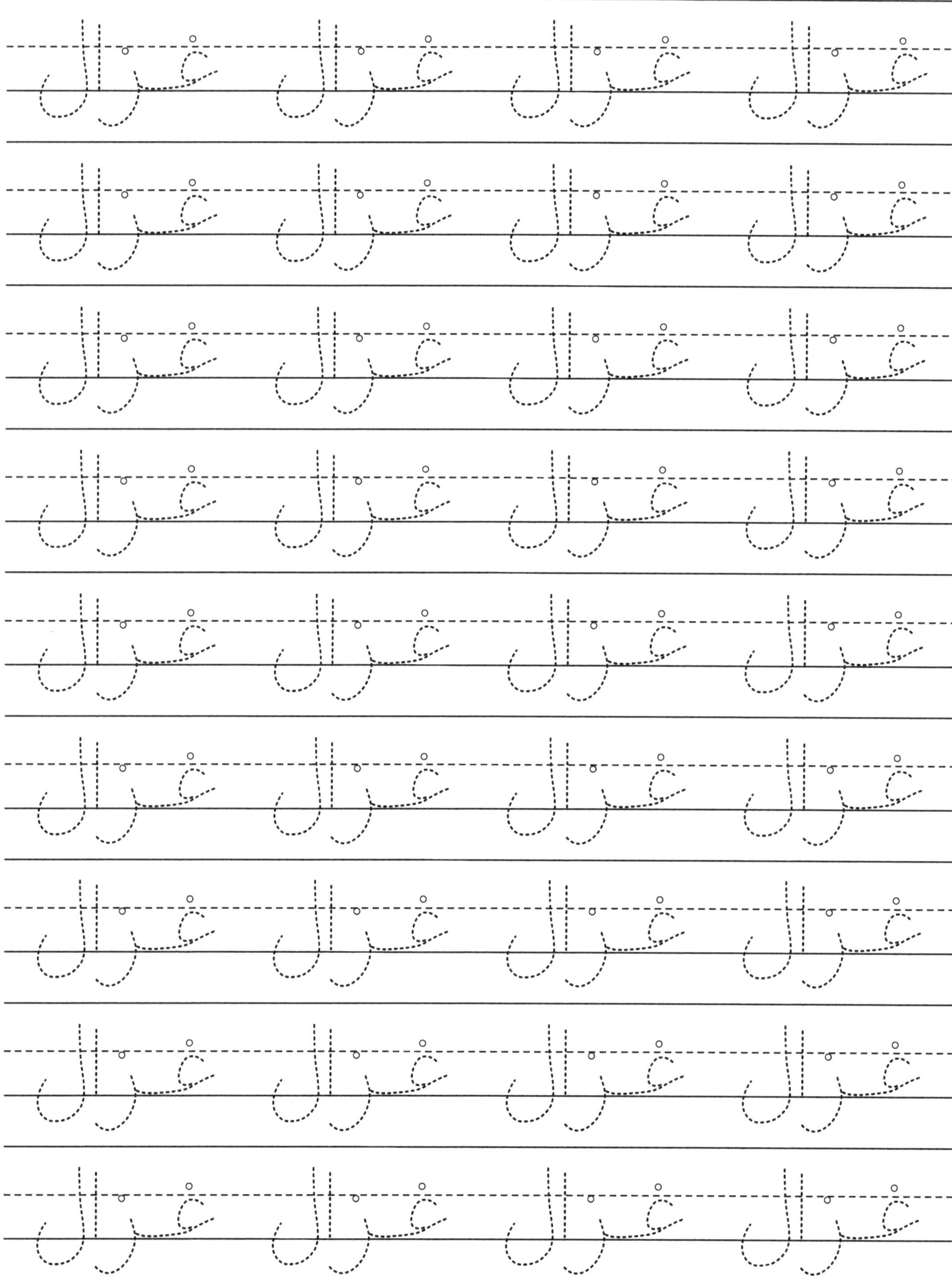

فيل

Elephant	**FAA** - ف

ف ف ف ف ف ف ف ف

ف ف ف ف ف ف ف ف

ف ف ف ف ف ف ف ف

فيل فيل فيل فيل فيل

فيل فيل فيل فيل فيل

فيل فيل فيل فيل فيل

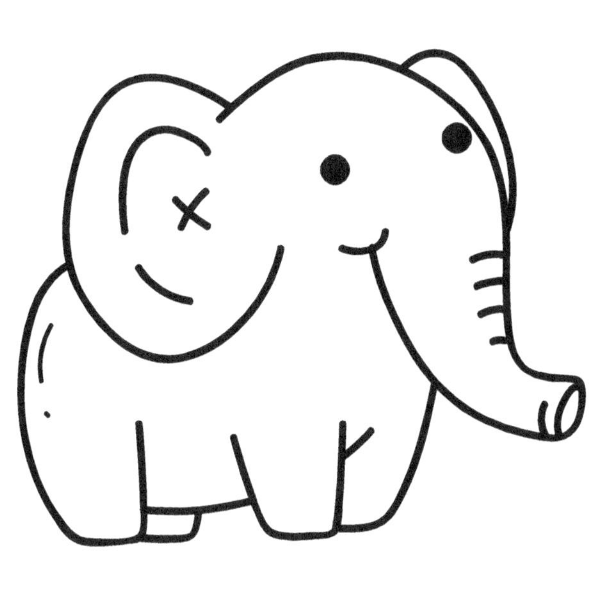

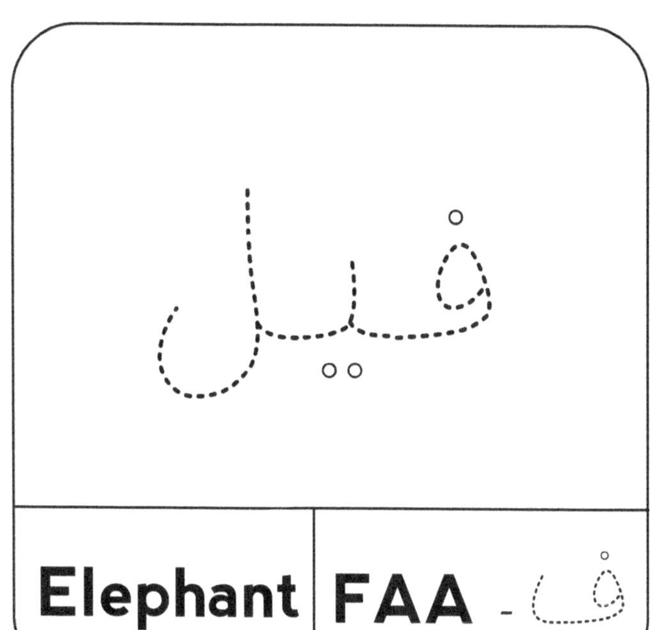

Cat
QAAF - ق

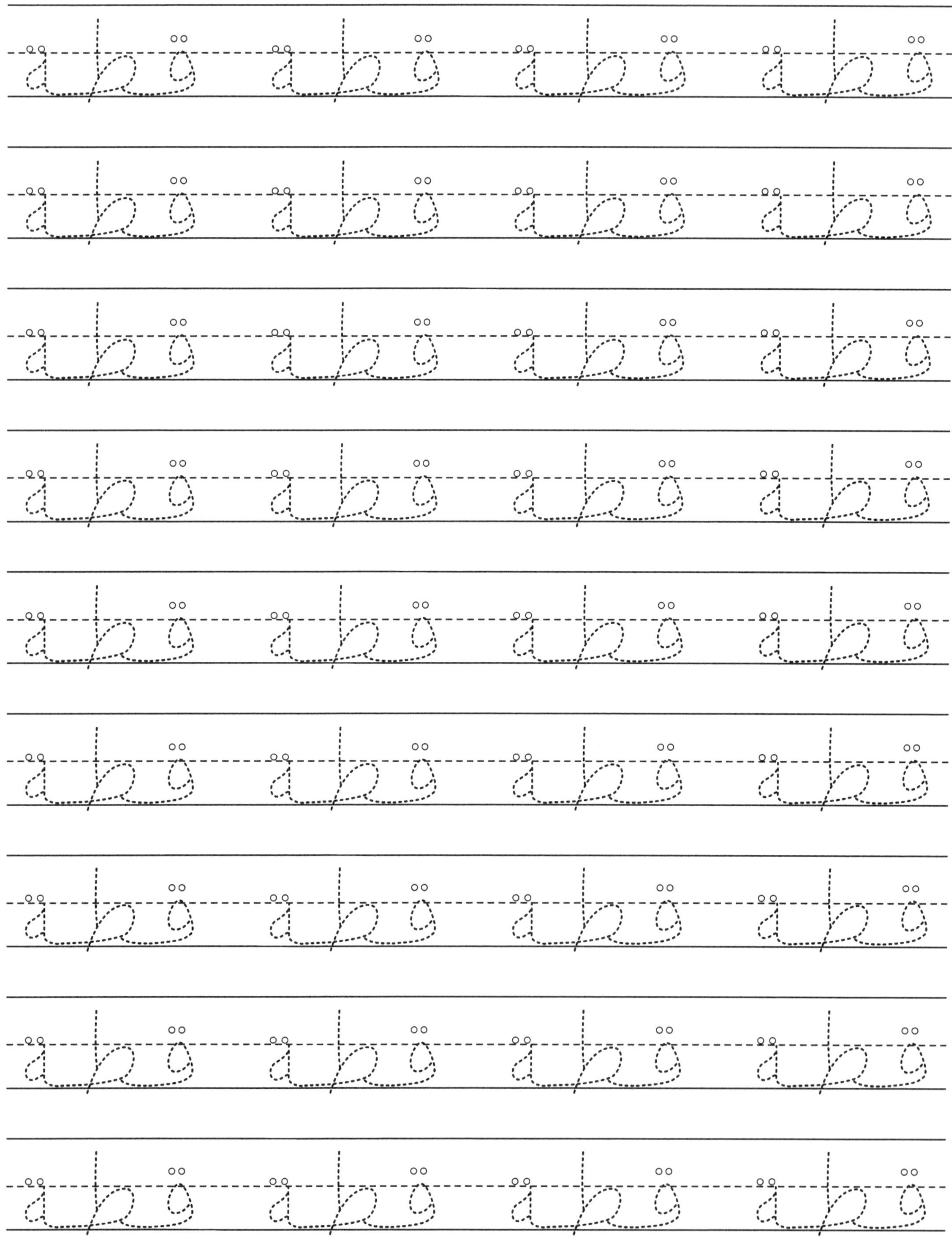

Dog | **KAAF** - كـ

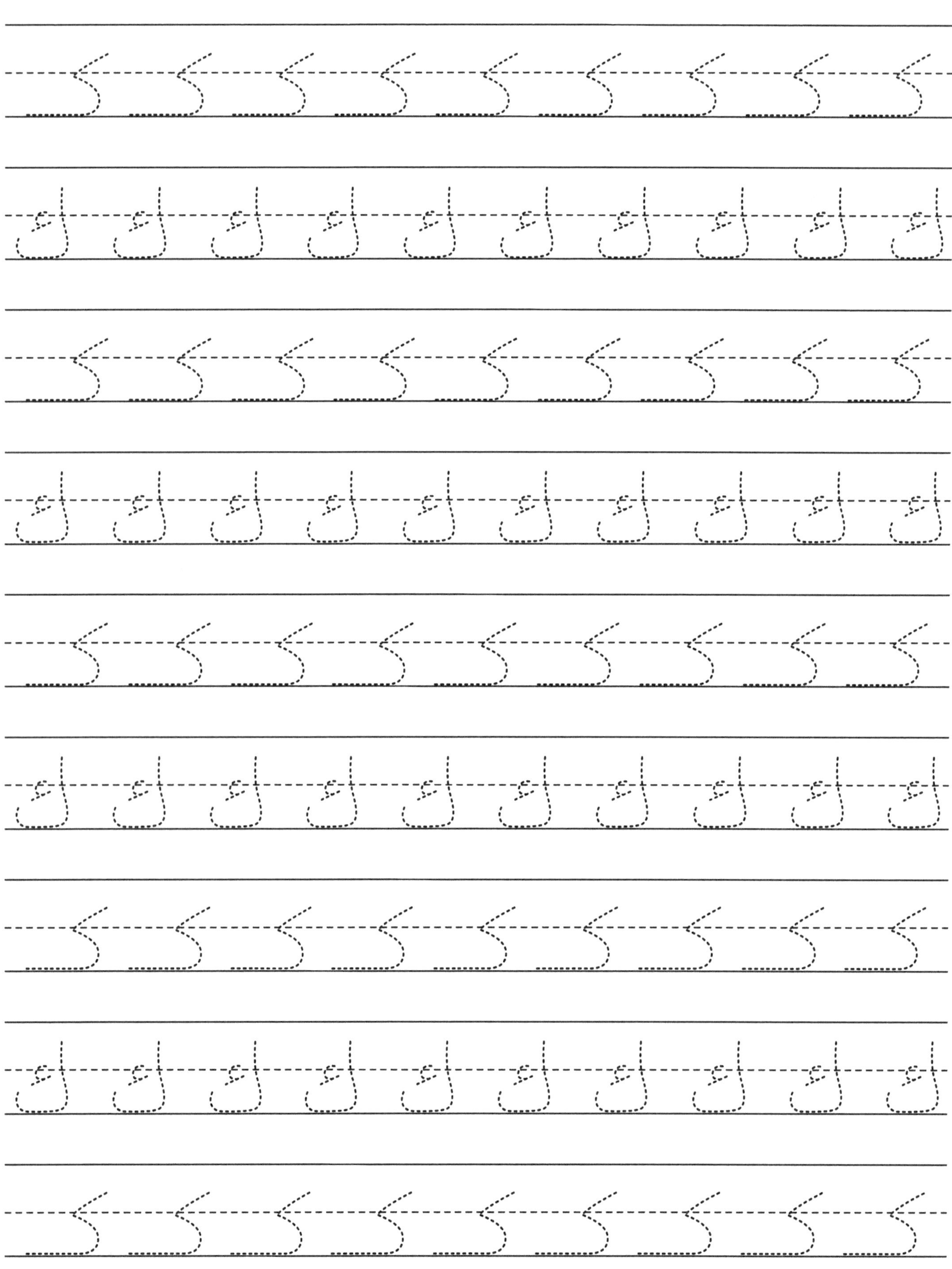

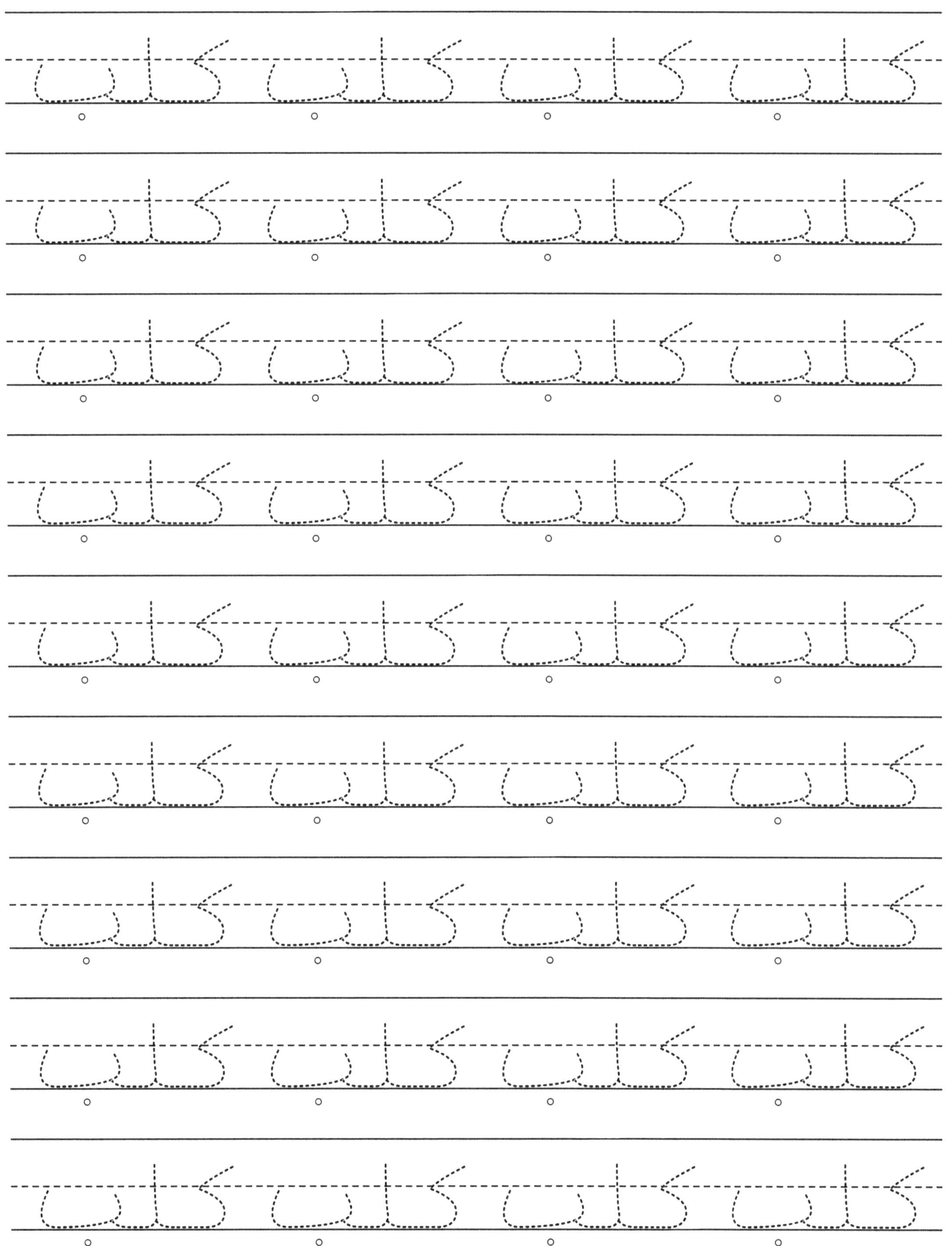

لاما

Lama | **LAAM** - ل

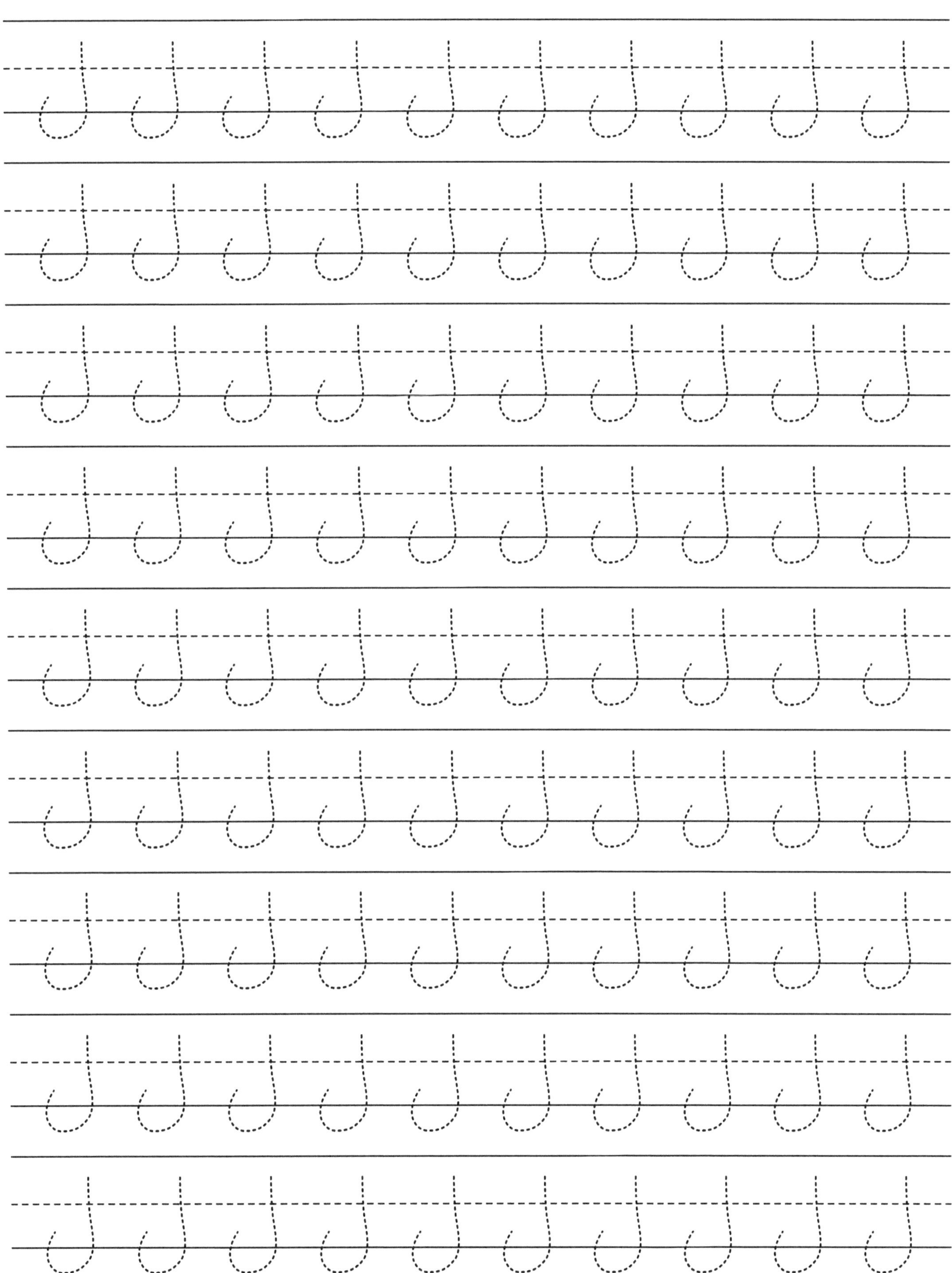

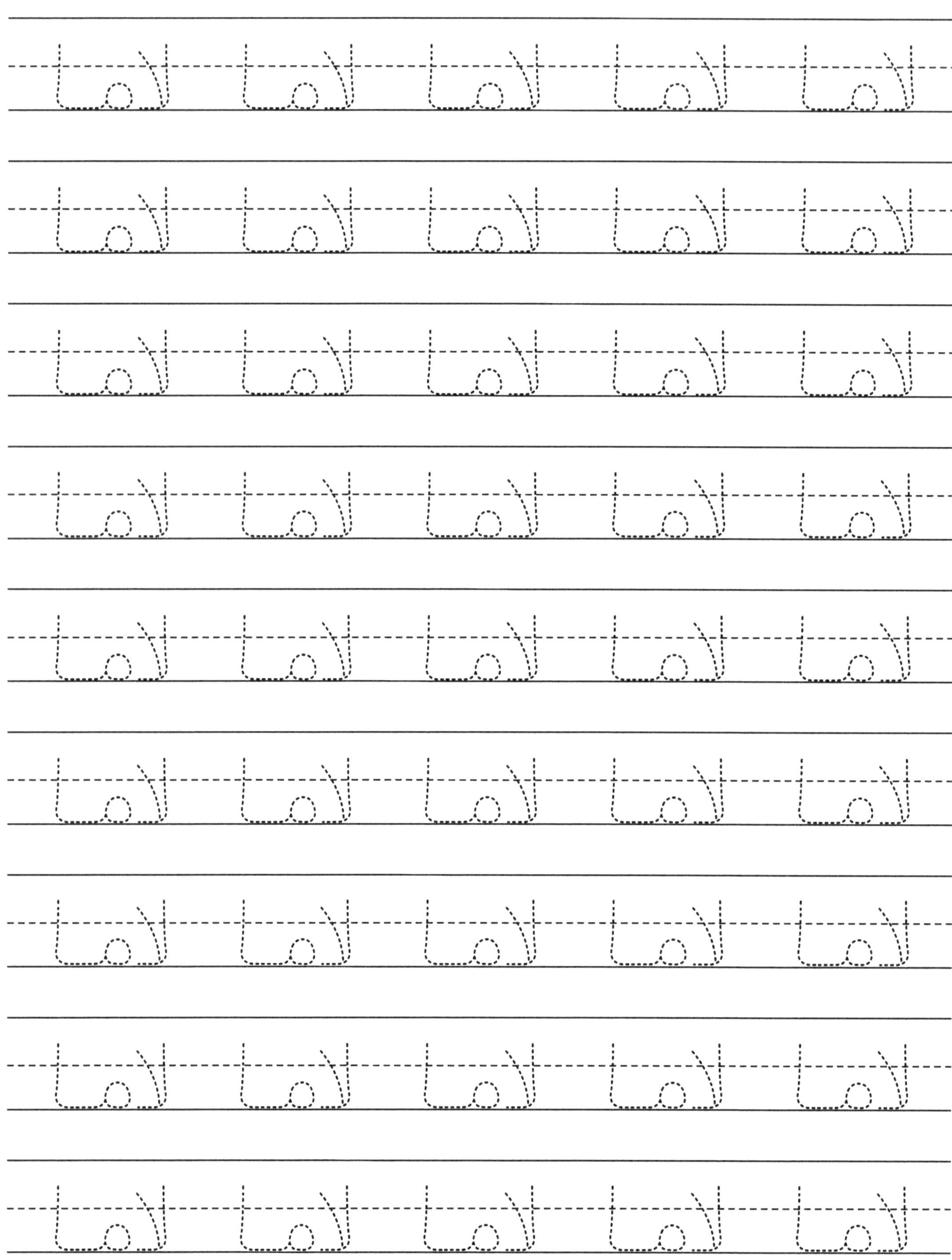

Goat
MIIM - م

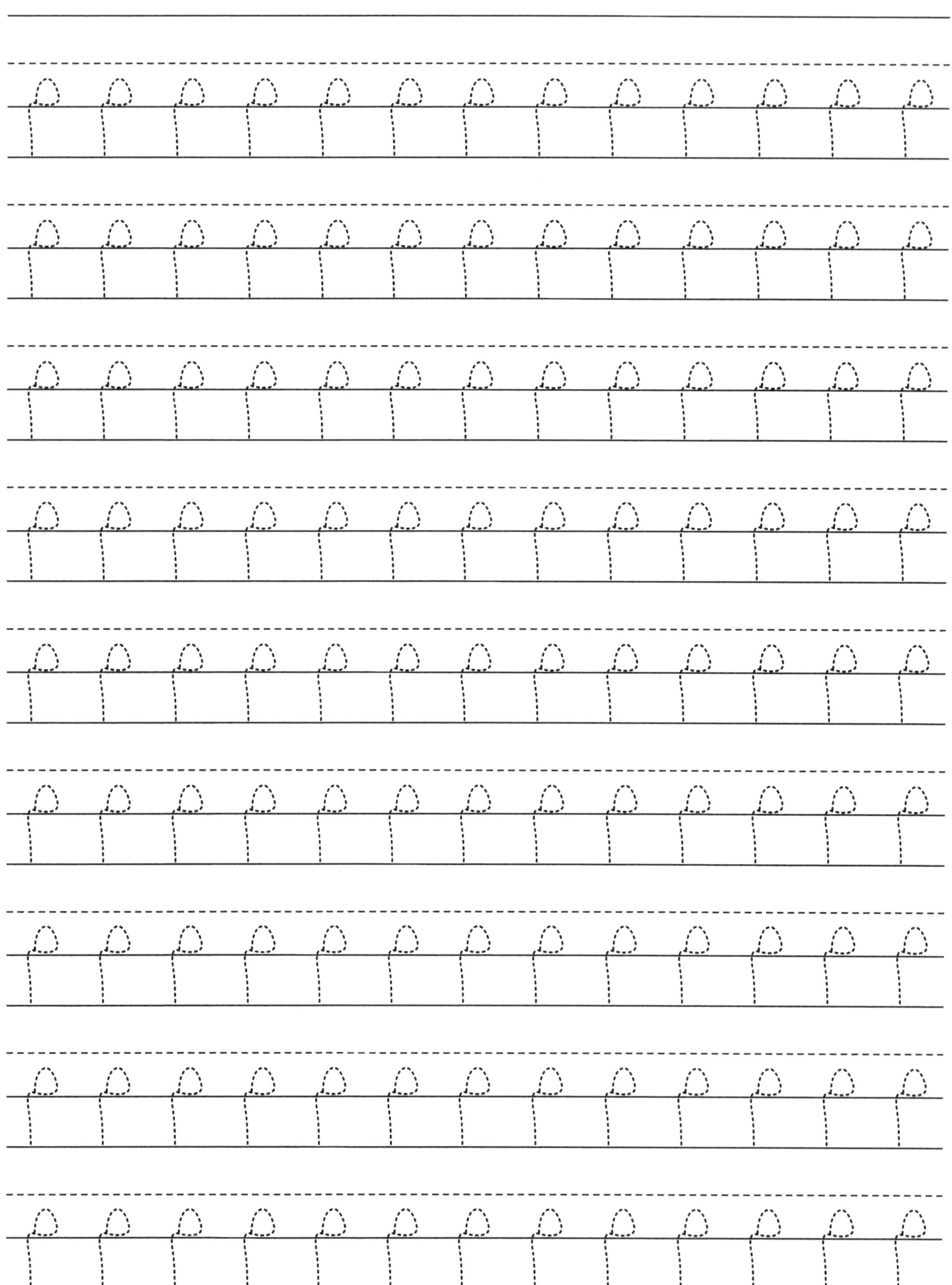

نحلة

Bee	NUUN - ن

ن ن ن ن ن ن ن ن ن

ن ن ن ن ن ن ن ن ن

ن ن ن ن ن ن ن ن ن

نحلة نحلة نحلة نحلة

نحلة نحلة نحلة نحلة

نحلة نحلة نحلة نحلة

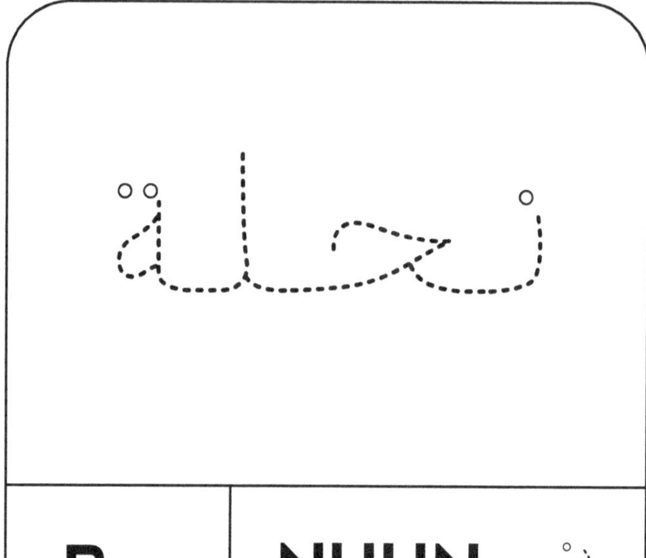

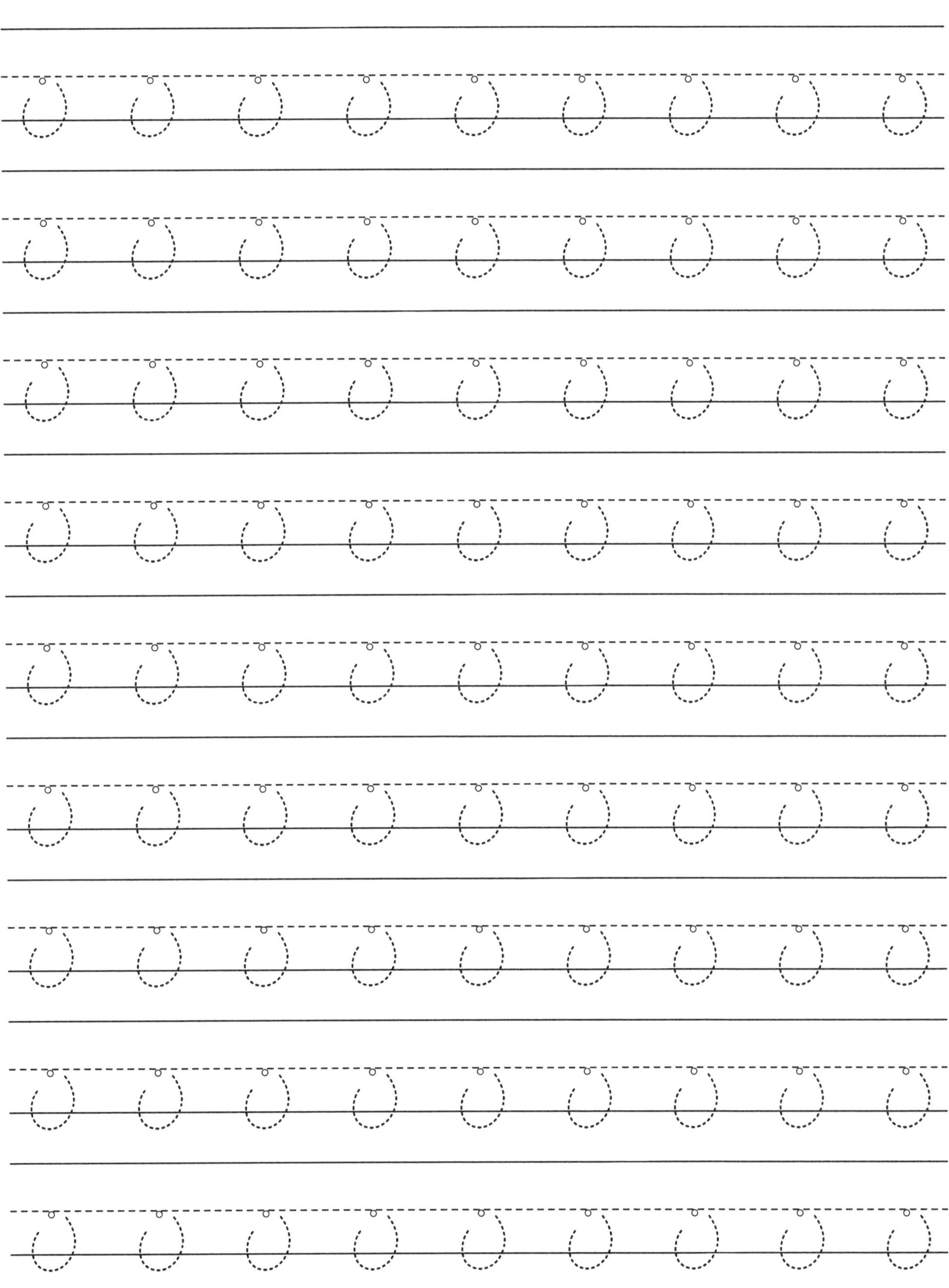

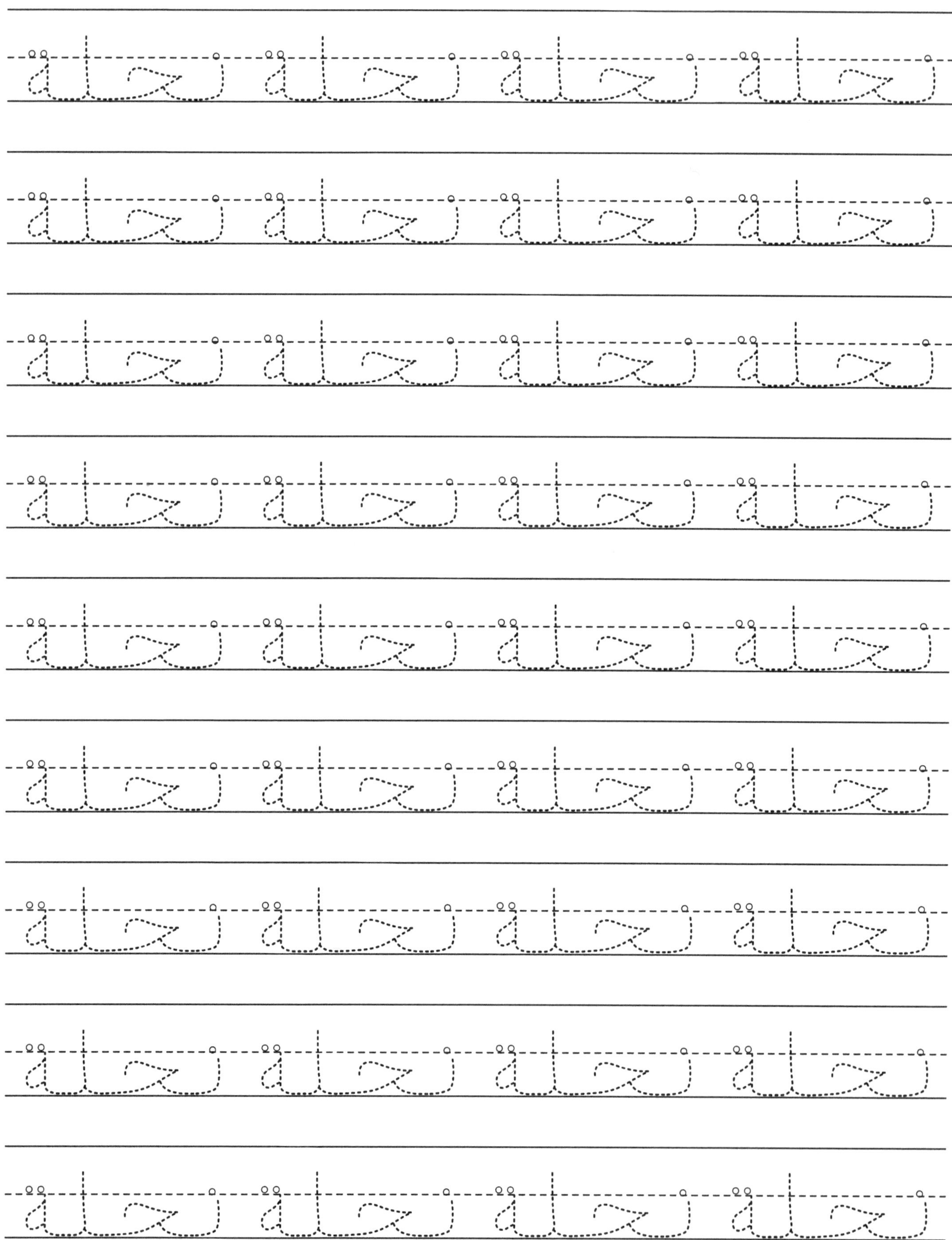

هدهد

Hoopoe	HAA - ـه

ـه ـه ـه ـه ـه ـه ـه ـه ـه

ـه ـه ـه ـه ـه ـه ـه ـه ـه

ـه ـه ـه ـه ـه ـه ـه ـه ـه

هدهد هدهد هدهد

هدهد هدهد هدهد

هدهد هدهد هدهد

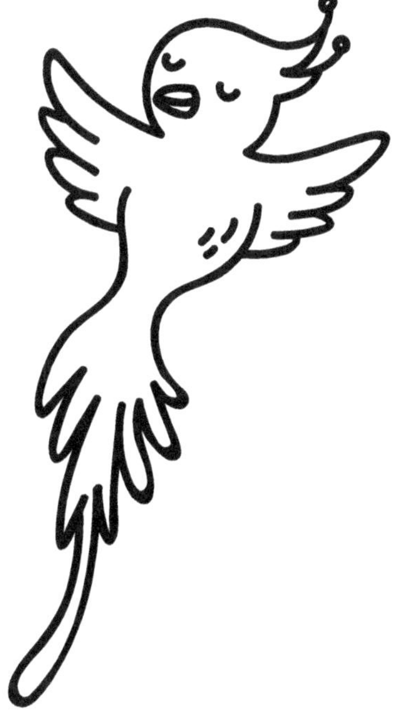

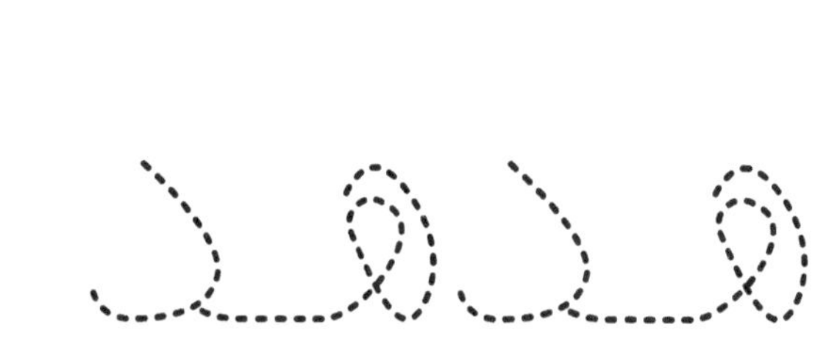

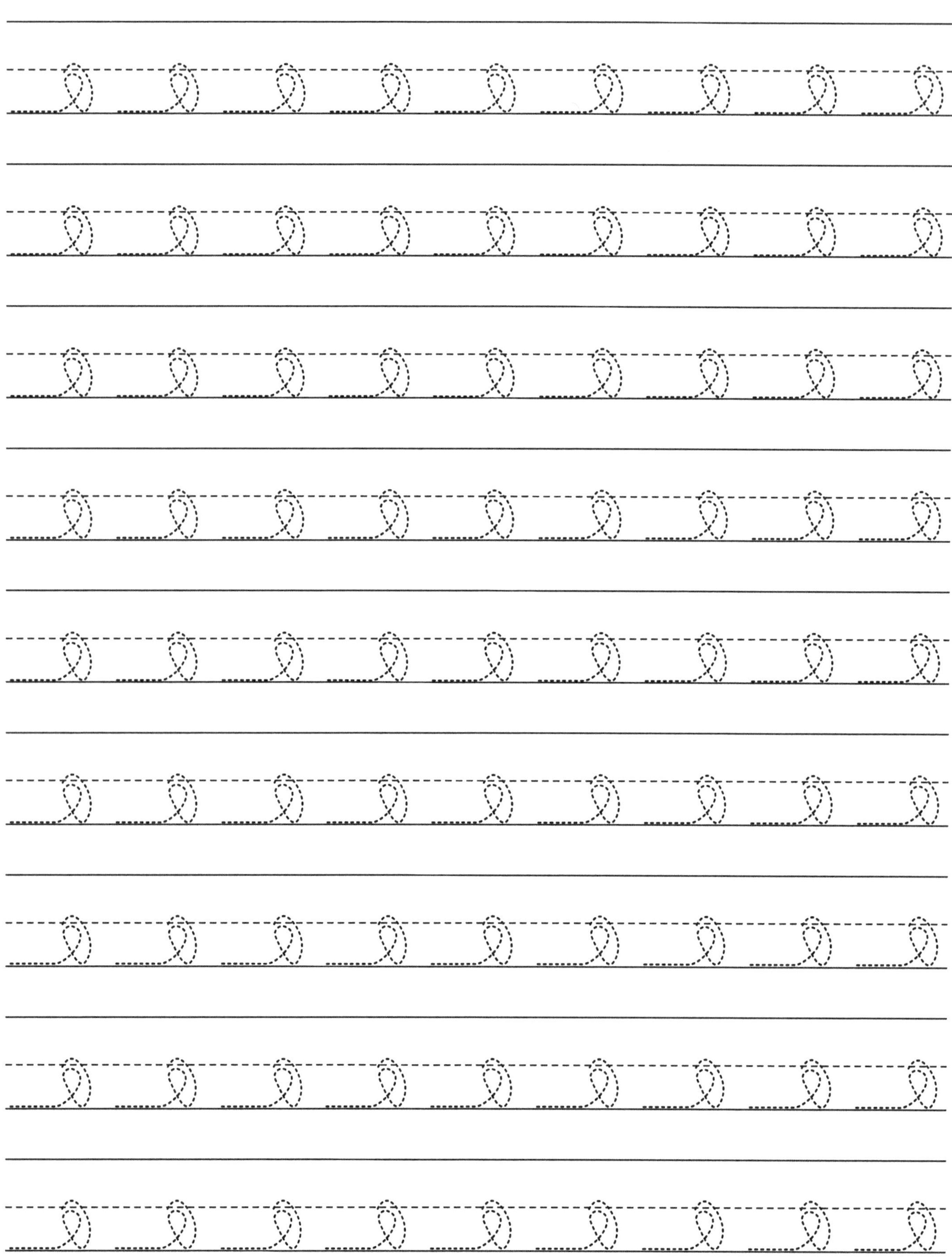

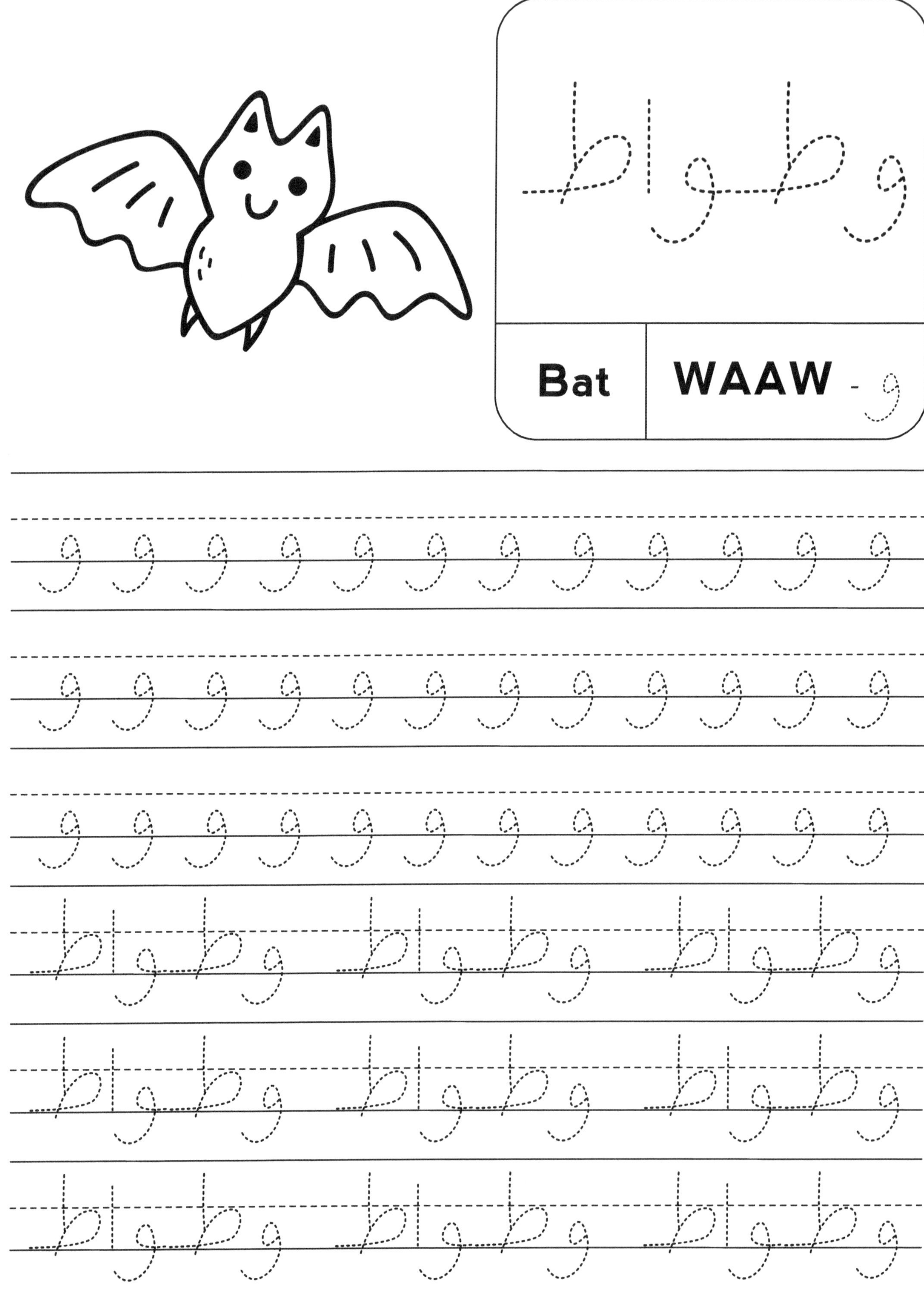

Bat
WAAW

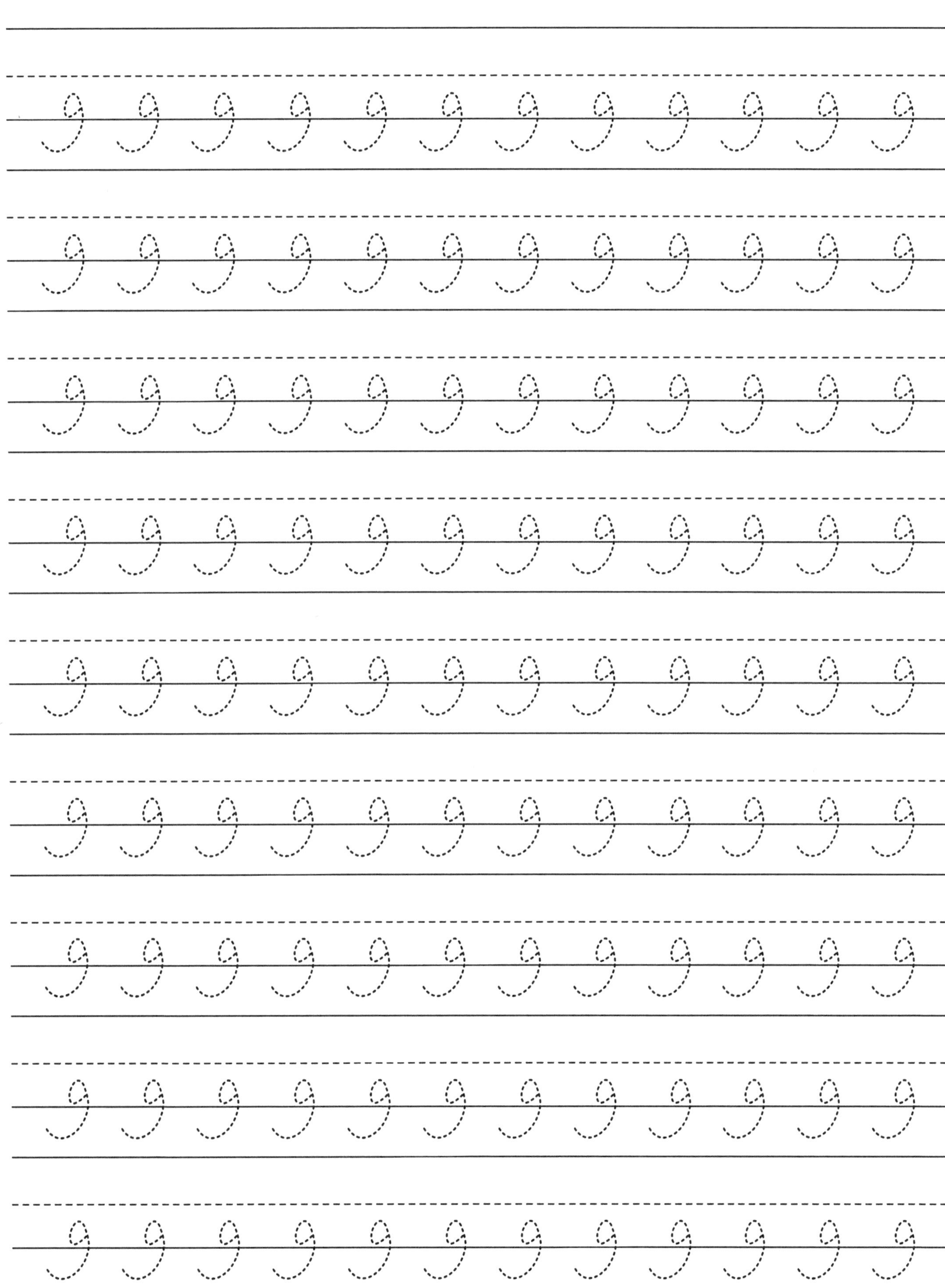

يمامة

Dove | **YAA** - ي

ي ي ي ي ي ي ي ي ي

ي ي ي ي ي ي ي ي ي

ي ي ي ي ي ي ي ي ي

يمامة يمامة يمامة

يمامة يمامة يمامة

يمامة يمامة يمامة

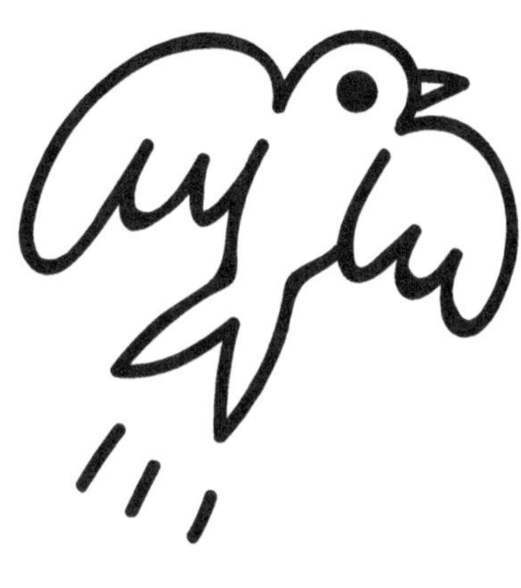

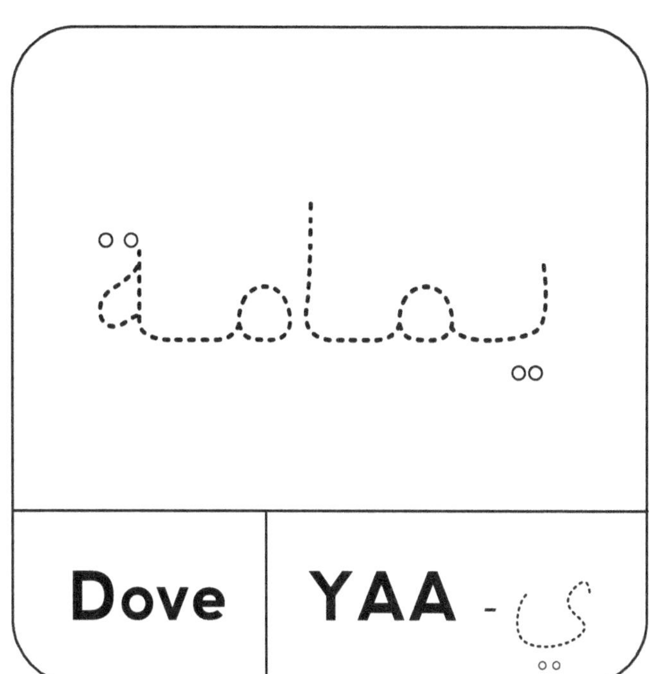

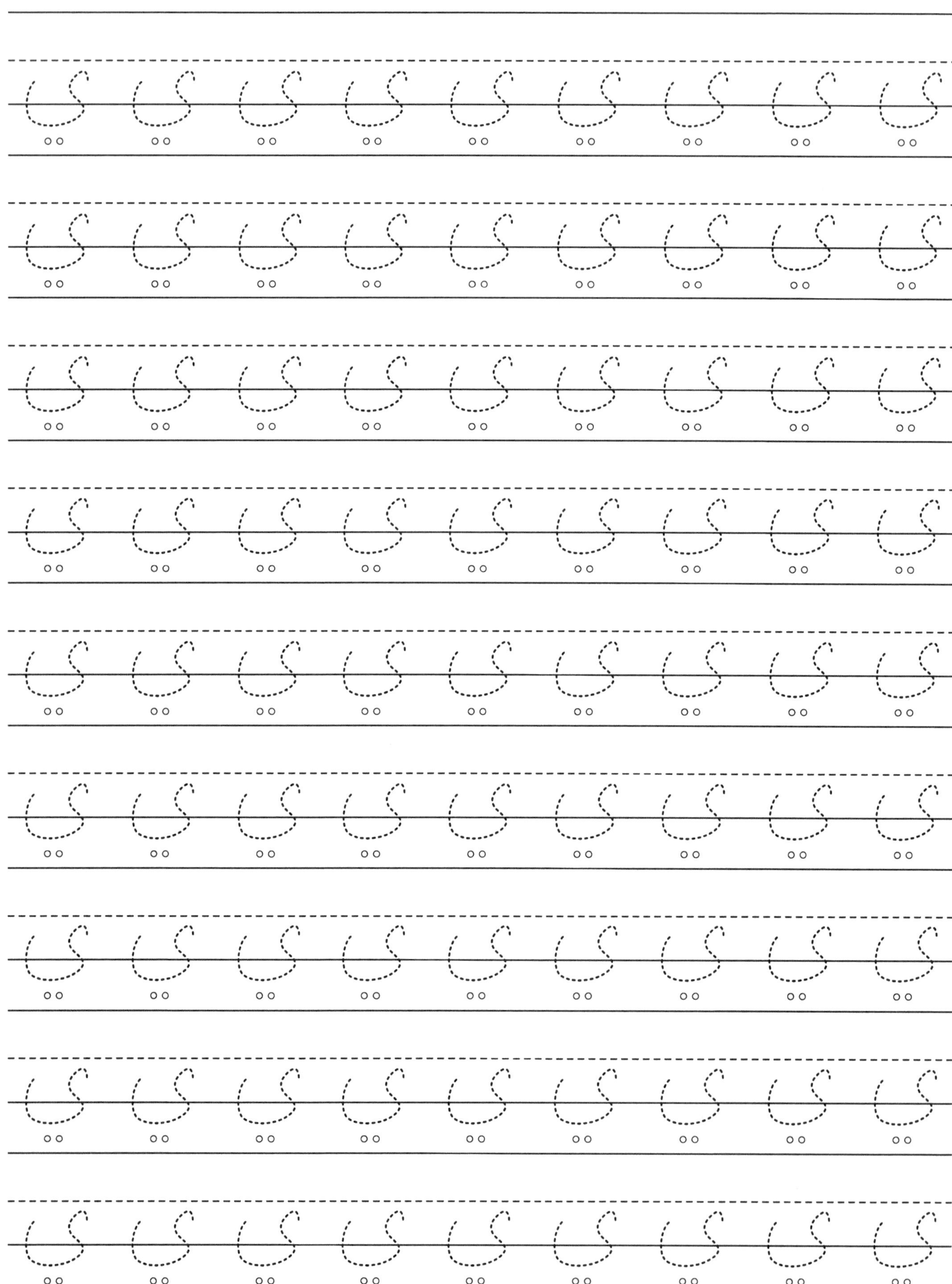

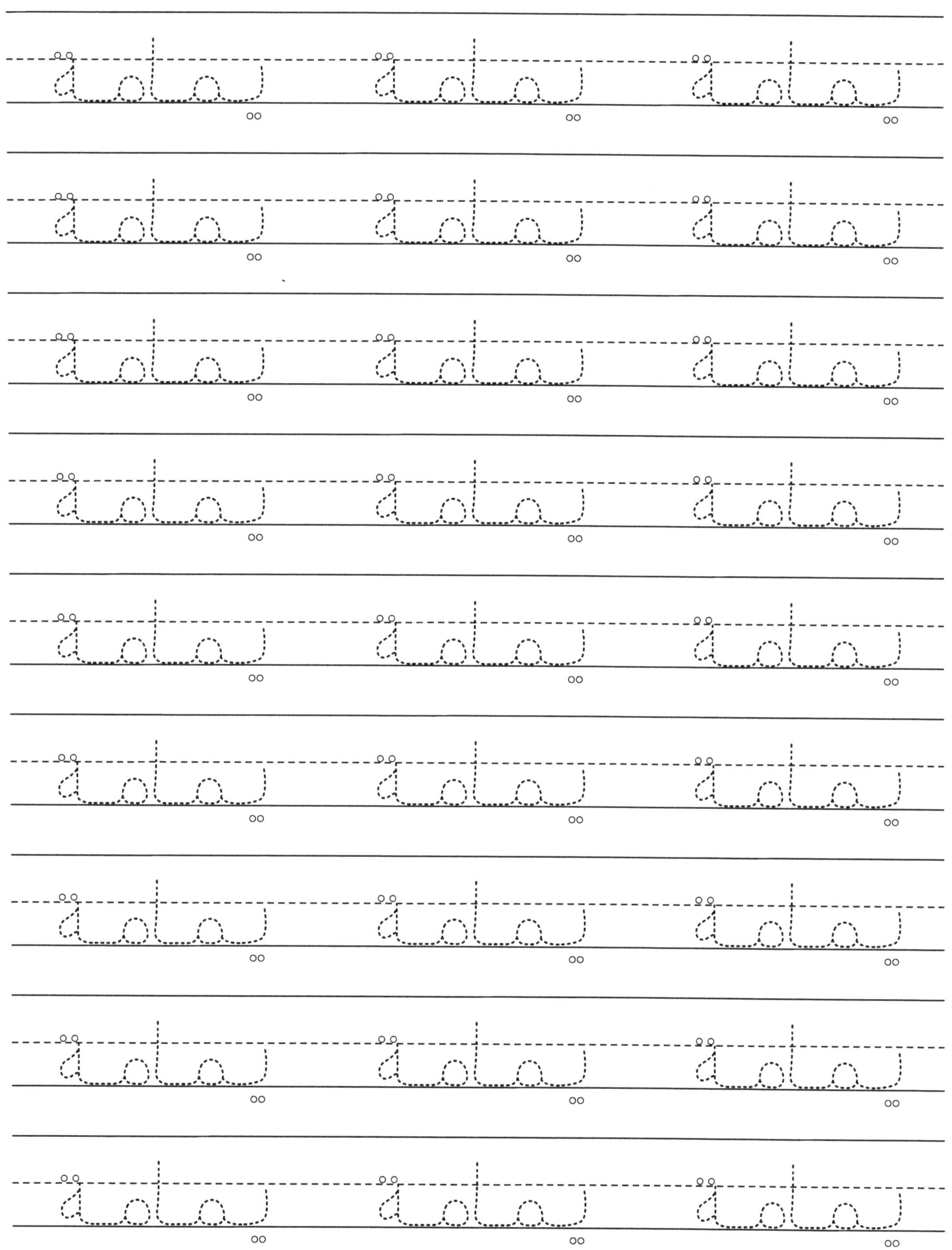

www.ingramcontent.com/pod-product-compliance
Lightning Source LLC
Chambersburg PA
CBHW080845160726
47999CB00009B/3016